'Where do the concepts of ego, self, person, and subject come from, and what presuppositions of knowledge do each and every concept invoke? Often used interchangeably without awareness of the theoretical, clinical, ethical, and even legal impasse as created by disenfranchising their terms from the traditions where they emerge, the specified application of the Ego, the Self, the Subject, and the Person are as endemic to English-based general therapeutic practice as they are to the Anglo-Saxon Lacanian transmission.'

Tamara Dellutri, *Lacanian psychoanalyst; founding member of Lacan/UK; member, Foro del Campo Lacaniano de México, IF-EPFCL*

'Raul Moncayo's interrogation of the concept of individual in psychoanalytic theory explores the notions of the "Ego," the "Self," the "Subject," and the "Person" as they operate within a Freudian–Lacanian ethics and clinical practice. Historically, these terms have remained confused in the psychoanalytic literature and have been utilized inconsistently across Jungian, object relational, critical theoretical, and Lacanian traditions. Moncayo provides a comparative analysis of the religious, philosophical, and psychoanalytic conceptions of these four terms while distilling along the way their specific place in the Lacanian clinic. Not merely a theoretical exposition, *The Concept of the Individual in Psychoanalysis* continues Moncayo's "return to Lacan" by constructing a theory that situates the dynamic operation of these four aspects of the individual in Lacanian thought.'

Carlos A. Jimenez, *PsyD, Psychological Associate; LSP, San Francisco*

The Concept of the Individual in Psychoanalysis

The Concept of the Individual in Psychoanalysis considers the different conceptions of the individual that are found in psychoanalysis according to the culture in which it operates, and its political structure.

Considering the origins and use of concepts including the Ego, the Self, the Subject, and the Person, Raul Moncayo considers Lacanian analysis together with Freudian and Jungian theory, philosophy, and religion. Moncayo expands on the concepts in different cultures and political structures, including English, French, German, and Chinese. The book also considers the concept of the self as used by Winnicott, Kohut, and Lacan.

The Concept of the Individual in Psychoanalysis will be of great interest to psychoanalysts in practice and in training, and to academics and students of Lacanian and psychoanalytic studies.

Raul Moncayo was born in Chile and first trained as a psychoanalyst in Buenos Aires. He obtained his PhD in social-clinical psychology at the Wright Institute in Berkeley and trained as an analyst at the Lacanian School of Psychoanalysis, which he also helped found. He is the founder of the Chinese American Center for Freudian and Lacanian Analysis and Research.

Routledge Focus on Mental Health

Routledge Focus on Mental Health presents short books on current topics, linking in with cutting-edge research and practice.

Titles in the series:

Life Skills and Adolescent Mental Health: Can Kids Be Taught to Master Life?
Ole Jacob Madsen

Gender, Sexuality and Subjectivity: A Lacanian Perspective on Identity, Language and Queer Theory
Duane Rousselle

Lacan, Jouissance and the Social Sciences: The One and the Many
Raul Moncayo

Understanding and Coping with Illness Anxiety
Phil Lane

The Linguistic Turn of the English Renaissance: A Lacanian Perspective
Shirley Zisser

The Concept of the Individual in Psychoanalysis: The Ego, the Self, the Subject, and the Person
Raul Moncayo

For a full list of titles in this series, please visit https://www.routledge.com/Routledge-Focus-on-Mental-Health/book-series/RFMH

The Concept of the Individual in Psychoanalysis

The Ego, the Self, the Subject, and the Person

Raul Moncayo

LONDON AND NEW YORK

First published 2025
by Routledge
4 Park Square, Milton Park, Abingdon, Oxon OX14 4RN

and by Routledge
605 Third Avenue, New York, NY 10158

Routledge is an imprint of the Taylor & Francis Group, an informa business

© 2025 Raul Moncayo

The right of Raul Moncayo to be identified as author of this work has been asserted in accordance with sections 77 and 78 of the Copyright, Designs and Patents Act 1988.

All rights reserved. No part of this book may be reprinted or reproduced or utilised in any form or by any electronic, mechanical, or other means, now known or hereafter invented, including photocopying and recording, or in any information storage or retrieval system, without permission in writing from the publishers.

Trademark notice: Product or corporate names may be trademarks or registered trademarks, and are used only for identification and explanation without intent to infringe.

British Library Cataloguing-in-Publication Data
A catalogue record for this book is available from the British Library

ISBN: 978-1-032-8-34351 (hbk)
ISBN: 978-1-032-8-34375 (pbk)
ISBN: 978-1-003-5-09349 (ebk)

DOI: 10.4324/9781003509349

Typeset in Times New Roman
by Apex CoVantage, LLC

Contents

Introduction: The Predecessors: The Hindu Self and
Non-Self in Chan Buddhism   1

1   The Phenomenology of the Person   3

2   Social Structural Versus Liberal Theories
    of the Individual   5

3   The Repressed-Repressive Unconscious   9

4   The Structural Theory: The Arousal of the
    Super-Ego, from the Soil of the Id   13

5   Ego Psychology   19

6   The Jungian Theory of the Self   21

7   The Lacanian Subject   23

8   The Symbolic and the Imaginary   37

9   The *Je* and the *Moi*, the Ego, and the Subject   49

10 Freud's and Lacan's Early Ego   53

11 The Self in Winnicott and Kohut   67

12 Uses of the Concept of the Individual in Psychoanalysis 69

13 The Ego or Subject of the Real 71

Index *73*

Introduction
The Predecessors: The Hindu Self and Non-Self in Chan Buddhism

The ancient Hindus (6,000 BCE) believed in an eternal self/soul that is purified and blessed in each lifetime through the practice of Yoga. Shakyamuni Buddha, the founder of Buddhism (500 BCE), changed this by saying that the One is a mind (psyche = soul) but not an eternal soul or a Self. The sacred elements are always changing and not eternal. Not only there is no-soul but also no-self. What is the holy and the sacred if not a divine soul and self?

The One is empty in its own being. Being is non-being, or Being is emptiness, and emptiness is free of definition. However, emptiness is light, and light speaks without a self and as an illuminated subject. The subject is a word or signifier, the ego is an imaginary fantasy, and the Real ego is a form of Other jouissance. The Hindu 'I am That' of Hinduism is changed to 'I am This,' "or I am as a form of luminous and blessed jouissance, that is both me and my ideal teacher or G-d or *Shandi* as the source of light." The 'I am That' of Hinduism has become the 'I am This' of Chan Buddhism. In Mandarin Chinese, *Ben Wo* is ego, and *Ben Ta* is 'It' or the empty subject.

Lacan's teaching is not only a philosophical, religious, or scientific theory. Lacanian thought is a school of wisdom, or a knowledge of jouissance. Lacanian thought converges with science and religion or *re-ligare*. Atheism can be the same as non-theism. Psychoanalysis links religion, philosophy, and science.

1 The Phenomenology of the Person

Phenomenology is the study of subjective experience.

The ego is both the person, and an agency or instance within the psyche. In the imaginary of the specular image or body image, it appears as a unified persona. The social is the unified persona which in Christian countries represents the social norms, and the identification with Christ (ego ideal).

Husserl's concept of the person is a multilayer structure not unlike Freud's psychical apparatus. Not much difference there. In Heidegger's existentialism the person just means Dasein or existence, consciousness, or mind. The person as a form of mind is nothing else than the Jungian persona, a failed attempt to become whole. It is not a form of true self since it represents keeping up with appearances. This is a form of frivolity and not the authenticity that Heidegger speaks about linked to finding and speaking in one's own voice. This is the full speech that both Heidegger and the early Lacan speak about. Intentionality of consciousness is transformed by Freud into the intentionality of the Unconscious.

Phenomenology and the humanistic Marxism of the young Marx presents a critique of relating to another human being as an object. Phenomenology, humanism, and existentialism accept treating the human being as a subject but not as an object. 'Objectification' is to use other subjects as objects and commodities. From this ethical point of view the entirety of Freudian psychoanalysis could be rejected. Psychoanalytic theory and nature are required for the use of the concept of the other as object of desire. A subject as an object is something special or *agalmic*, not a fetish, but a true jewel. An object does not represent alienation or exploitation. The object is understood empirically via subjective experience and not objectified through statistical methodology.

References

Husserl's (1999). *Basic Writings in Transcendental Phenomenology*. Bloomington: Indiana University Press.

Mark, K. *Writings of the Young Marx on Philosophy and Society*. Cambridge: Hackett Publishing Company. 1967.

2 Social Structural Versus Liberal Theories of the Individual

In mathematics and arithmetic, the first number is either zero or one depending on the number system and the cultural historical reference. Every number is a unit/trace, and in contemporary mathematics 0 is included in each number of set theory.

In a unary number system, starting with zero, three is the fourth number. In the natural number system, without a zero concept, three is the third number.

Three is the third cultural number needed to mediate the natural biological relationship between mother and child (two). So then there's a question of cultures that begin with zero (Indian) and cultures that begin with one (Europe). Zero-based cultures are based on the values of negation and renunciation and compassion, and love for the other. One-based cultures are based on love of the individual I and the political autonomy of the ego. The ego stays outside the socialization imposed by society and remains close to Nature (however, defined).

Compassion is not the same as what Freud called 'Universal Love' which disgusted him because of what he saw as its defensive nature in relation to hate. However, Freud acknowledged that there are many forms of love. There is eros and agape like in Plato. Compassion is $a$sexual, unlike love that can be sexual. Now we have discovered that animals and apes also experience love linked to parenting and not to sex.

Analysts can also experience this kind of love and compassion that is not based on countertransference or empathy and has therapeutic effects. Lacan never dropped any of the students that he knew were going to leave him before they left of their own accord. Lacan experienced rejection but not his students. Lacan spared his students of the rejection, although he was both idealized and rejected by his students.

DOI: 10.4324/9781003509349-3

The Third in Hegel's Dialectic

The subject in Hegel is overdetermined by the Other of society that gives subjects their social freedom. The subject is opposed to Nature and becomes a second nature or antithesis only through negation, that then yields the synthesis of the Spirit.

In formal logic, a proposition is either true or false. The false helps arrive at the true, but without constituting a truth in itself. In probability theory, the truth only represents a probability that a proposition has a percentage of being true. In order to be true, a proposition has to be at least 50% true (0.5), or at least a half-truth and a half-fiction; 1 is completely true, and 0 is false.

For formal logic, a fiction is something false, while for dialectical logic a fiction is a form of truth or can lead to truth. In dialectical logic, truth is a third element as a form of synthesis. In negative dialectics, in contrast to the Hegelian dialectic, the synthetic element falls off, and what takes its place is the overall structure that includes formal and dialectical logic. Negative dialectic drops the ambition of dialectical knowledge of gaining or achieving an absolute form of knowledge that is not falsifiable because its truth remains not in the relative Symbolic, but in the different order or dimension of the Real (Truth of jouissance). Jouissance as truth can be relative (fusion with the mother, phallic jouissance [intercourse]), or absolute: the Third Other jouissance.

In Hegel there are three elements in knowledge: thesis, antithesis, and synthesis. The third element synthesizes the previous two into a new proposition. In the negative dialectics of Adorno, the synthetical element disappears because consciousness does not produce synthesis, only the unconscious does. In this sense the unconscious represents a more legitimate, therapeutic form of 'unknown knowing' (*l'insu qui sait*).

This was Freud's response to Assagioli (2000), the founder of psychosynthesis. Assagioli thought that analysis divided rather than healed the psyche, so he asked Freud why synthesis did not play a bigger role in the practice of interpretation in psychoanalysis. Freud responded by saying that he does the analysis first, and then the unconscious realizes the synthesis.

In quantum theory, energy waves in the void generate both particles and identical anti-particles with reverse charge that are not synthesized, only that in rare occasions the + particle is not destroyed, and matter is created out of its replication and differentiation. Not a dialectic. Creation comes from the destruction of a particle by an anti-particle, which sometimes survives. The first is positive charge, the second negative, and the third positive, but it is not a dialectic. The creative charge survives and goes from death to life, or from nothing to something.

The Marxist Dialectic

The subject is in a contradiction within capitalism. The liberal subject is supposed to be free but is everywhere in chains (Marx, 1967). This in fact was proven to be wrong by history. Both the capitalist and the worker became rich. Consider the example of contemporary China. Both the capitalist and the worker enjoyed surplus work and value.

The Third in Peirce and Linguistics

For Peirce the interpretant or interpretation of a sign/representation is a second representamen or representation. The first or primary representation for Peirce represents an object, the meaning of which is given by a second representation/signifier. For Peirce semiosis is a triadic process. The first is a signifier or representation, the second is the object in the world, and third is the element of interpretation, or interpretant. In Peirce there is the 'no-thing' in itself in his Triad, in contrast to Lacan. For Lacan, the object world is produced by the signifier, and the thing itself remains outside the signifier as a form of jouissance that can be both pleasurable and painful.

For Peirce, the object and the interpretant are two correlates of the sign: the one being antecedent, the other consequent of the sign. The problem with Peirce's theory of the sign is that it conceives of an original relation between the sign/representation and the object, as if the sign had derived from a quality of the object instead of the signifier determining the meaning of the object world.

References

Assagioli, R. (2000). *Psychosynthesis*. Esalen Books.
Hegel, G. H. (1831). *Phenomenology of Spirit* [*Phänomenologie des Geistes*], translated by A. V. Miller. A Manual of Principles and Techniques. Oxford: Oxford University Press, 1977.
Marx, K. (1967). The German Ideology. In: *The Marx and Engels Reader*. New York: Norton and Company.

3 The Repressed-Repressive Unconscious

In the metapsychological papers, Freud (1901) distinguished among three forms of the Mind: Consciousness (Cs.), the Preconscious (Pcs.) or the descriptive Unconscious, and the repressed Unconscious. In his paper on the mystical writing pad, Freud distinguished between the Cs. Pcs. System and awareness that remains free from memory and record. Between the systems there is a form of defense: suppression as a conscious form of repression, and unconscious repression that separates the Pcs. from the Ucs.

Freud's account of the vicissitudes of unmastered id cathexis which come into operation once more through the ego ideal, does not in my opinion solve the puzzle of how the ego-ideal can be unconscious. First of all, Freud's example would only explain the existence of unconscious censorship in 'psychopathological' cases in which the Oedipus complex has not been successfully repressed and mastered. Such instances would represent the failure of the secondary process. Successful sublimation is more than a repression in that it destroys the Oedipus complex according to Freud. Contrary to this, the experience of dreams teaches us that the phenomenon of unconscious censorship goes far beyond the order of psychopathology.

We need a concept of the Symbolic and of repression and censorship and the law as intrinsically tied to this order in the unconscious. The structural laws of the symbolic as mechanisms of the law and the unconscious as transcurring unconsciously and as forms of desire simultaneously. The law itself can be repressed as seen in the disavowal of perversions, the foreclosure of psychosis, in obsessions (self-reproaches), and the sexual seductions of hysteria. The voice of the Symbolic, the I or subject of the signifier is also the Other as judge and super-ego, as the law, and the desire of the Other, and unconscious desire.

See the following for examples of the repression of the super-ego.

Secondly, Freud himself concedes that it is only the cathectic energy of the ego-ideal which comes from the id but not the censoring ideational content of the ego-ideal itself. The super-ego is acquired from without and in this sense it is not primal. Freud never resolved the contradiction between positing the super-ego as a differentiation of the drives and as being derived from the external social world. Furthermore, not only does the fact that the energy of the super-ego is derived from the id not explain the unconscious nature of repression but also (as I will show) the idea that repression is the task of the super-ego contradicts Freud's idea that the ego itself is the agent of repression.

I have already resolved this problem by formulating the hypothesis that the super-ego is the source of morality within the ego and the part of the ego which is unconscious. Yet Freud thought of the ego and the super-ego as two different agencies. This is the reason why it is difficult to understand why Freud introduces the concept of the super-ego as a way of solving the puzzle posed by an unconscious part of the ego.

The ego and the super-ego are seen by Freud as the two separate parties of a master-servant, sadist-masochist relationship. The distinction between the ego and the ego ideal is based on the fact that, although the ideal is differentiated out of the ego, the ego can also enter into the relation of an object to the ego ideal.

> We have been driven to the hypothesis that some such agency [the ego-ideal] develops in our ego which may cut itself off from the rest of our ego and come into conflict with it.
> (Freud, 1923, p. 52)

Freud offers some clues in the direction of a possible solution.

> We know that as a rule the ego carries out repressions in the service and at the behest of the super-ego; but this is a case (the unconscious sense of guilt) in which it has turned the same weapon against its harsh taskmaster.
> (1923, p. 52)

Because the super-ego is cathected with the energy of the id belonging to repressed ideas and therefore is a substitutive formation, the ideational contents of the super-ego itself can fall prey to repression.

Here the mechanism by which the sense of guilt remains unconscious is easy to discover. The hysterical ego fends off a distressing perception with which the criticisms of its super-ego threaten it, in the same way in which it is in the habit of fending off an unendurable object cathexis – by an act of repression (idem, p. 51).

If the ego can turn against the super-ego the same weapon it uses against the id on behalf of the super-ego, then it follows that the super-ego or the conscience at work in the ego can also be repressed. The unconscious part of the ego is unconscious because it is repressed.

References

Freud, S. (1901). *Metapsychological Papers*. Strachey, J., Freud, A., Strachey, A. & Tyson, A. (1957) The Standard Edition of the Complete Psychological Works of Sigmund Freud, Volume XIV (1914–1916).

Freud, S. (1923). *The Ego and the Id*. New York: Bantam.

4 The Structural Theory

The Arousal of the Super-Ego, from the Soil of the Id

With the second theory, Freud personalizes what in the first theory of mind were structural symbolic effects. Lacan emphasizes that defenses take place within language and within the functions of metaphor and metonymy as described by Jakobson (1956 and 1990). A metaphor substitutes for something else in the same way that a symptom does, except that in the symptom there is a quantum of jouissance that is displaced onto the substitute. We say yes when we intend to say no, or vice versa. There is a metonymical displacement from no to yes, as well as a metaphoric substitution. At the same time, there is a change in sign in the quanta from positive to negative, from pleasure to pain. Pleasure and pain are not symmetrical since pleasure can be experienced in both increases and decreases of tension while pain is only experienced with an increase in tension or pressure.

Metaphors and ideals guide and censor (the direction of sense) thought rather than the ego being the source of censorship. In Freud's second theory it is unclear whether the unconscious ego is the super-ego or whether the super-ego and ego both have conscious and unconscious dimensions. If the latter is the case, then what is the difference between the unconscious ego and the unconscious super-ego in terms of the function of unconscious defense? This in fact is difficult if not impossible to ascertain and it points to a dead end in the second theory of mind and personality.

Paradoxically, the agency of the subject is limited to the act of leaving empty the place of ego-agency within the structure and the place of the cause of desire within the subject. On the other hand, the larger agency, the autonomy, and activity of the Symbolic could also represent the work of a benevolently depersonalized subject. The illusion is that the ego is the agent that advances and realizes things or symbolic causes but instead it is the Symbolic that advances and realizes the subject.

Freud was not satisfied with the therapeutic results of the first metapsychological theory of undoing repression in analysis and making the

14 *The Structural Theory*

unconscious conscious. He then focused on undoing the defenses that he came to understand as also unconscious but not repressed. The source of repression he attributed to an unconscious part of the ego, but he could not resolve how this differed from an unconscious super-ego as the source of repression. The unconscious super-ego can also suppress the unconscious ego. The punitive capacity interferes with the unconscious functioning of the ego.

Through his study of the process by which melancholics identify with and internalize their lost loved ones, Freud discovered that not only do children identify with their parents and their values (in the sense of the meaningful ideas which capture their affective, energic interest), but that these identifications are substitutions for desires which the children see themselves forced to renounce.

> An object which was lost has been set up again inside the ego, that is, an object cathexis has been replaced by an identification. This kind of substitution has a great share in determining the form taken by the ego and it makes an essential contribution towards building up what is called its 'character.'
> (Freud, *Mourning and Melancholia*, 1917, p. 28)

The significant point here is that identifications are substitute formations erected in the place of abandoned id desires or id cathexes or object choices. "The character of the ego is a precipitate of abandoned object cathexes, and it contains the history of those object-choices" (p. 29). The ego is a vicissitude of the sexual drive. Now it is important to notice why these object-choices have been abandoned and the nature of what remains in their place. Otherwise, Freud's statement can be somewhat equivocal. It can entice one to think that character has a biological nature and is the direct derivative of id-object-choices. In what way is character a precipitate of the id if the id and the child are all fantasy, restlessness, fleeting impulsiveness and limitless desiring and character means moderation and self-control?

Freud initially in describing the process by which an ego is formed does not stress or clarify enough the reasons why id-object choices are abandoned and transformed into identifications. He only comes to account for this when he begins to address the formation of the super-ego in connection to the constitution and resolution of the Oedipus complex.

Furthermore, Freud does not differentiate between the identifications which compose the ego and those which constitute the super-ego. He writes as if the movement by which objects are set up within the ego were a single process. Not only that, but the whole theory is brought to bear upon the problem of the super-ego.

The notion of character as a precipitate within the ego is meant to explain the nature of the super-ego. It is difficult to discern within Freud's discourse which identifications concern the ego itself and which modify the ego in the direction of the ego ideal.

The only distinction that Freud introduces is that between a primary kind of identification with the parents which "is a direct and immediate identification" which "takes place earlier than any object cathexis," and a later one based on the renunciation of an object-choice, and which comes to reinforce the primary identification. But this distinction cannot be used to shed light on the difference between an ego and a super-ego identification because Freud (1913) sees even this early primary identification as a basis for the ego ideal.

> This leads us back to the origin of the ego-ideal; for behind it there lies hidden an individual's first and most important identification, his identification with the father in his own personal prehistory.
> (p. 31)

Therefore, although it is not possible to differentiate within Freud's theory between an ego and a super-ego 'identification' (ego-ideal), there seems to be two types of identification which in Freud's view contribute to the formation of the ego-ideal. The first one appears to precede even the distinction between object libido and narcissistic libido since according to Freud the identification took place prior to any object cathexis, and he also relates the transformation of object libido into narcissistic libido to an abandonment of sexual aims.

This transformation and the abandonment of sexual aims has to do with the formation of the super-ego or ego-ideal as a normative function.

It should be emphasized that the nature of the primary identification and its role in the function of the ego-ideal still remains a mystery to be solved. Perhaps Lacan's concept of the mirror stage can be an aid in this direction.

I mentioned that the reason why objects are abandoned and transformed into identifications, and object libido is transformed into narcissistic libido, is intrinsically related to the formation of the ego-ideal.

Along with the demolition of the Oedipus complex, the boy's object cathexis of his mother must be given up; the object cathexes are given up and replaced by identifications. The authority of the father or the parents is introjected into the ego, and there it forms the nucleus of the super-ego, which takes over the severity of the father (or mother) and perpetuates his (or her) prohibition against incest, and so saves the ego from the return of the Oedipal object cathexis (1924, p. 176).

Thus, it is clear that through the super-ego something is affirmed (identification with parental prohibitions) and something is negated (libidinal object cathexis); but what is still unclear is the way in which the prohibitions of the super-ego arise from libidinal object cathexis. For as Ricoeur has noted, the novelty of Freud's theory of conscience does not reside so much in recognizing the social externality of authority, as in conceiving internal authority as a differentiation within the nature of desire and the drives.

Freud argues that due to the incest prohibition the child's erotic desires for the mother and/or father need to be given up. Their place may be filled by either a mother or a father identification. However, Freud does not specify with what aspect of the parent the child will identify or how this identification is internally related to the desires that have been abandoned.

Freud suggests that the identification may take place along gender lines. The male identifies with the father, the female with the mother. But if this were the case in the 'positive complex' the abandoned object of desire or the parent as an object of erotic desire will not be introduced into the ego. The theory fails in this respect.

It will be only in the inverted (homosexual) complex that the child will replace an object cathexis for an identification. For example, let us paraphrase Freud and assume that the female had an ambivalent object relation towards the mother: on the one hand she perceived her as a rival in relation to her desire for her father; on the other hand, the mother herself due to constitutional bisexuality was an erotic object choice and the father was perceived as a rival.

Where for whatever reasons the masculinity is stronger in the female and the hostility towards the father and the erotic desire for the mother are felt more acutely; the feelings belonging to the positive complex (hostility towards the mother and sexual desire for father) coalesce and are replaced by an identification with the father. Conversely, in the heterosexual (positive) complex the rivalry and the erotic object relation which belong to the inverted complex coalesce and are replaced by an identification with the mother.

Thus, in the inverted complex, heterosexual desires are given up while in the positive complex homosexual desires are the ones that are given up. Therefore, it is deducible that the formula which describes object cathexis as given up and transformed into identifications is not one that can be immediately generalized to all object cathexes as Freud usually does.

> For this super-ego is as much a representative of the id as of the external world. It came into being through the introjection into the ego of the first objects of the id's libidinal impulses—namely, the two parents. In this process the relation to those objects was desexualized; it

was diverted from its direct sexual aims. Only in this way was it possible for the Oedipus complex to be surmounted.
(1924, *The Economic Problem of Masochism*, p. 167)

In the case of the male child the relinquishment of the libidinal object relationship with the mother does not produce an identification with the mother. The heterosexual boy identifies with the father and this identification results not from giving up the desires for the mother but from giving up the desires toward the father.

> The father-identification will preserve the object-relation to the mother which belonged to the positive complex and will at the same time replace the object-relation to the father which belonged to the inverted complex: and the same will be true mutatis mutandi of the mother-identification.
> (1923, *The Ego and the Id*, p. 34)

The identification with the father might develop along the lines of the ideas advanced in *Totem and Taboo* (1913).

This remorse (for the killing of the primal father) was the result of the primordial ambivalence of feeling towards the father. His sons hated him, but they loved him too. After their hatred had been satisfied by their set of aggression, their love came to the fore in their remorse for the deed. It set up the super-ego by identification with the father; whether one has killed one's father or has abstained from doing so is not really the decisive thing. One is bound to feel guilty in either case, for the sense of guilt is an expression of the conflict due to ambivalence and of the eternal struggle between Eros and the death drive.

The hostility is suppressed by strengthening the opposite feeling of love through an identification which then results in the formation of the ego-ideal. This, as far as I can tell, would be the meaning of the father identification being a replacement for an id-object cathexis towards the father.

In *The Ego and the Id*, with the introduction of the ego-ideal, the concept of sublimation becomes intrinsically related to the problem of identification. It is through identification that Oedipal impulses are sublimated and put to work to serve the ego-ideal which then becomes the agency which executes the repressions.

References

Freud, S. (1913). Totem and Taboo. In: *The Standard Works of Sigmund Freud*. London: Hogarth Press.

Freud, S. (1917). Morning and Melancholia. In: *The Standard Works of Sigmund Freud*. London: Hogarth Press.
Freud, S. (1923). The Ego and the Id. In: *The Standard Works of Sigmund Freud*. London: Hogarth Press.
Freud, S. (1924). The Economic Problem of Masochism. In: *The Standard Works of Sigmund Freud*, vol. XIX. London: Hogarth Press.
Jakobson, R. (1956). The Metaphoric and Metonymic Poles. In: *Metaphor and Metonomy in Comparison and Contrast*, edited by R. dirven and R. Porings, revised ed. Berlln: de Gruyter, pp. 41–46.
Jakobson, R. (1990). *On Language*. Cambridge: Yale University Press.

5 Ego Psychology

The English are empiricists, and North Americans are pragmatists. They prefer a simplified, almost atheoretical, mostly clinical version of psychoanalysis. They are anti-philosophical. Fairbairn in his object relations version of ego-psychology produces a simplified and vulgar version of psychoanalysis. German and Romance language cultures are more theoretical.

The general uses of the ego concept are as a subject of experience or one's own person; as self-consciousness, as a group of neurons, or ideas.

In ego psychology the ego is defined as a system of functions: reality testing, perception, memory, thinking, attention, judgment and a function of control, adjustment, and integration linked to the frontal cortex of the brain. The ego is an expression of the binding power of Eros and works with sublimated, desexualized, or quiescent energy.

Ego is the competence that is formed in social-symbolic interactions, identifications with symbolic rules which are secured by growing individuation and independence. Ego-ideals and ethical ideals beyond preconventional and conventional morality culminate in abstract ethical principles which are logical, comprehensive, and universal.

Jesus is an example of Kohlberg's postconventional morality. To the defiler of the sabbath Jesus said, "Man, if indeed thou knowest what thou doest, thou art blessed; but if thou knowest not, thou art cursed, and art a transgressor of the law." Freud said that when faced with a difference of opinion those who appeal to conventional authority or dogma, whether religious or scientific, work with their memory rather than with their reason.

Rational independence is different than both an id rebellion and a super-ego conformity and conventionality. An ethic beyond instrumental and critical reason is doing something for no particular reason, a senseless act for the act itself, beyond altruism and egoism. Doing something for nothing is being a waste product, a good-for-nothing, paying for nothing

DOI: 10.4324/9781003509349-6

and being paid for nothing, which is the most expensive thing. The symbolic works most effectively when the ego of profit, gain, and utility gets out of the way. This sets forth a surplus and constructive form of jouissance that is a great stimulus and profit for the economy.

Reference

Kohlberg, L. (1983). *Moral stages: a current formulation and a response to critics*. Basel, NY: Karger.

6 The Jungian Theory of the Self

Jung divides the mind/psyche into collective unconscious, the personal unconscious, the ego, and the Self. According to Jung, women represent evil or the fourth element of the Christian trinity. For Freud there was no so-called personal unconscious because the individual unconscious is simply a permutation of the collective structure. Analysis is called personal, in the sense of private and confidential, not that it is individual. At the same time how each subject experiences the structure is unique, although this uniqueness is not the mask that a person pretends to be which is Imaginary.

Speech and images speak through us or through the *Je*. In addition, the concept of Jungian androgyny is like Freud's concept of unconscious bisexuality; however, androgyny differs from sexual difference and the concept of symbolic castration which requires a difference between the sexes. Sameness is not enough. The relation between the sexes also requires necessary difference. But difference by itself is also not enough. Sameness is also required, although this depends on how identity is defined. Identity represents equality more than subservience, surrender rather than submission; and always links identity with difference.

However, for Jung, correctly in my opinion, the higher ego-functions always remain functions of the Unconscious as a bigger, larger, if not higher, psychical principle. Instead of ego, he utilized the concept of Self to describe this state of affairs. The Self is a *complexio oppositorum* and an underlying union of opposites, a whole or totality including the conscious and the unconscious, the good and the bad, the rational and the irrational.

The Unconscious does not have a substance or a property of its own, other than being a type of process, or psychic form of impermanence. The Unconscious is not an entity or a mechanical hydraulic apparatus, or a machinic or cybernetic unconscious, although it is organized by structure as these systems are. The Self is inconceivable except in the form of symbols, mythical visions which are a range of human experience beyond

DOI: 10.4324/9781003509349-7

reason. Such symbols have a healing or curative dimension. Ethical function is a way to self-knowledge. Ethics is grounded in the Self rather than the ego. The Self seeks the unknowable rather than the knowable, the unknown meaning rather than a known uniformity of meaning. Self represents the unconscious and the ego consciousness. Obviously, this Self (or the Unconscious) is not narcissistic, as the ego is. Jung would say that the Self also has a relation to the Shadow, but then we're back to the Freudian ego.

For the ego there is a temptation to identify with the Self and the result is ego-inflation. Instead of being the Self without self-consciousness, people identify the Self with the ego. The less mindful we are of the Unconscious, the greater the danger that the ego will usurp the place of the Unconscious.

Lacan attempts a similar conceptualization with his notion of a science of the subject centered on an analysis of the Unconscious.

Jung's theory could be symbolized by the formula: S=O, where S stands for the Big Self and O stands for the Bionian Infinite or the Unconscious. Lacan's theory would be symbolized by the same algorithm S=0 where O (the Other) stands for zero (S=O=0) thereby being equivalent to the formula $=O or $=8, where $ stands for the obliterated subject, the no-self, and 8 or double O stands for the Infinite number, the Other of infinite change and variation whereby all things, phenomena and activities in their own being, are empty or free of permanent selfhood.

The 8 would also stand for the Möbius strip quality of psychical functioning. The Unconscious stands as a psychical, metapsychological topology wherein inside and outside, conscious and unconscious, are relative, dialectical terms. Inside and outside, self and other no longer function as strict binary opposites. All these possible and necessary logical relations and permutations constitute the alpha and omega of a subjectivity in both its self and no-self forms, intersubjective and transsubjective, relative and absolute forms.

It is not the ego, which is capable of creative functioning; rather, it is ego consciousness (cs.) or self cs. which inhibits spontaneous, natural, and creative functioning. In this regard, Loewald, although a member of the school of ego-psychology, argued for understanding the so-called "higher functions," not with ego-psychology constructs but rather with positively defined metapsychological concepts. He regarded the primary process and desire as sources of creativity, renewal, and timeless forms of intuitive knowing (unconscious knowledge, or 'unknowing-knowing).'

7 The Lacanian Subject

Lacan uses the repressed unconscious, the descriptive unconscious, and the Lacanian Real unconscious. The Real unconscious appears in two forms: the first Real is awful, dreadful, and destructive, and the second Real creates harmony or accord. The second Real is what Lacan calls the Name of the Father emerging from the Real and the Sinthome. Bion also has O similar to both of Lacan's Real but differs from the Other of the symbolic unconscious which is linguistic. Bion does not have an analysis of language.

When the analyst renounces to be in the place of the ideal and does not respond to the demand of the analysand, then in that void the analysand's fundamental fantasies will become apparent. The analysand not only wants the analyst to tell him/her what to do or not do, a demand of a demand, but also demands that the analyst give him or her the signifier of the phallus, as well as the object of love and of the drive. Finally, the analysand also wants to become and give the analyst the object that the analyst desires, lacks, and needs. The analysand wants the analyst to demand this object from him/her, but the analyst refuses to do so.

Following Lacan, I use the permutations of the Cartesian *cogito ergo sum* to illustrate the three dimensions of the subject. "I think (I speak), therefore I am," represents the self-image and the imaginary ego. When utilizing social language, the *moi*, the ego, says, I think, I speak. As Fink (1997) has pointed out, when the ego says I speak, "What he means thus refers to a level of intentionality that he views as his own; it refers to an intentionality that fits in with his self-image" (p. 24). This is why Lacan made a conceptual distinction between the enunciating ego and the subject of the enunciation, and between meaning and signification.

Meaning is imaginary because "it is tied up with our self-image, with the image we have of who and what we are" (idem). Instead, the subject of the unconscious, of the Symbolic, of signification, and of the enunciation is conceived by Lacan as an effect of the operation of the signifier. The classical Freudian slips, the parapraxis, the double meanings, the polyvocal significations – in short, all of the formations of the unconscious are effects of the language-like symbolic structure of the unconscious.

Within a Lacanian framework it is the symbolic order (a set of laws, values, myths, etc.) and the order of language which establishes the structures and functions of the subject which in the ego-psychology school are attributed to non-defensive and "realistic" ego-functioning. For Lacan reality is a social construct given by the culture-bound and law-bound order of language. The rules of language and the rules of kinship (i.e., incest prohibition) are conceived as two fundamental and integral elements of culture.

In addition, the Other also refers to parental figures and figures of authority from whom the subject receives both social rules and the rules and content of language. Just as the ideal ego and narcissism are derivative objects of the desire of the mother, it is the relationship with the symbolic father which frees the subject from narcissism and from being an imaginary object of the mother's desire. The identification with the symbolic father establishes the subject as a pivot of the Symbolic and the Symbolic as a pivot of subjectivity.

Lacan's second Real generates a new Ego and a new unifying principle in which meaning can be enigmatic and beyond words. Finally, a third permutation of the Cartesian *cogito* brings to the fore the third dimension of experience: the register of the Real. The symbolic "I think where I am not" needs to be permutated into "I am where I do not think," which I interpret as signifying the realm of being or parabeing beyond thought, signification, and representation.

The subject is not the ego or the individual, and
Mind is not consciousness.

Isn't it striking that, by an extraordinary conjuring trick of history which can be taken as a step forward within a certain tradition of the development of thought, we have returned to a state of consciousness, which by any standard is not new.

We have used the term Copernican revolution to describe Freud's discovery. In relation to this conception, the Freudian discovery has exactly the same implication of decentering as that brought about by the Copernican discovery. Consciousness is not Mind. Mind=Unconscious. It is quite well expressed by Rimbaud's fleeting formula – poets, as is well known, don't know what they're saying, yet they still manage to say things before anyone else.

Lacan tells us that the unconscious completely eludes that circle of certainties by which man recognizes himself as ego. There is something outside this field which has every right to speak as I, and which makes this right manifest by coming into the world speaking as an I. It is precisely what is most misconstrued by the domain of the ego which, in analysis, comes to be formulated as properly speaking being the I.

The fact that he gave voice to this by calling it the Unconscious leads him to real contradictions in speaking of unconscious thoughts; he constantly apologizes for it. This is all terribly cumbersome since, from the point of view of communication, at the time he started writing he was forced to start off from the notion that what belongs to the order of the ego also belongs to that of consciousness. But that's not certain. If he says that, it is because of a specific stage in the development of philosophy which at that time assumed the equation ego=consciousness.

But the more Freud's work progressed, the less easy he finds it to locate consciousness, and he has to admit that it is in the end unlocalizable. Everything is progressively more organized within a dialectic in which the I is distinct from the ego. In the end, Freud gives the game up for lost – there must be, he says, conditions beyond our grasp here. The future will tell us what these are.

We will try to get a sense of how we can finally locate consciousness within Freudian theory. With Freud, a new perspective suddenly appears, revolutionizing the study of subjectivity and showing precisely that the subject cannot be confused with the individual (ego). I propose that the individual is dual, while the subject is an *indivitrio*, made of three elements.

Now what Freud's contribution was is the following: the manifestations of the subject in question can in no sense be localized on the axis of the intelligence, the excellence, the perfection of the individual. Freud tells us intelligence has nothing to do with the subject, the subject is not on the same axis: it is ex-centric. The subject as such, functioning as subject, is something other than an individual organism which adapts itself. It is something else from a specific number of cognitive and learning interests conceived of in relation to the individual.

We will confine ourselves to this topological metaphor for the moment – the subject is decentered in relation to the individual. That is what 'I is another' means.

The Ego of Narcissism

Possession at the level of the object is transformed into possession at the level of the ego as the peculiarity of self-love. Possession emphasizes that even those of our activities which seem to be most disinterested are motivated by the concern for glory, even passionate love (object cathexis already is narcissistic cathexis) or the most virtuous acts, however secret.

By engaging in so-called disinterested actions, we think we free ourselves from immediate pleasure and are seeking a higher good, but we are mistaken. For Freud, altruism is at bottom sheer egoism.

There is a hedonism specific to the ego. It is into this hollow, into this bowl, that the Freudian truth comes to be poured. You are deluded, no doubts, but the truth lies elsewhere. And Freud tells us where it is.

What then erupts, with the crash of thunder, is the sexual drive, the libido.

Freud first classified drives by introducing a distinction and a dynamic conflict between a self-preservation ego instinct and a libidinal sexual drive. He based this distinction on a larger difference between ego-libido, or interest in general, and object libido, or erotic desire. However, with the introduction of the concept of narcissism, ego libido became a vicissitude of the sexual drive. Thus, in the end Freud (1920) appealed to a distinction between a life drive and a death drive. Eros is defined as the tendency to preserve life and to join into ever larger units. Thanatos he defined as matter's tendency to return to a lifeless state.

In 1920, what may be called the last metapsychological period begins. For this period *Beyond the Pleasure Principle* is the primary text, the pivotal work. It is the most difficult. We won't resolve all of its puzzles right away. But that's how it happened: Freud first produced that, before elaborating his structural model [*topique*].

Analysts have complained that the *Beyond the Pleasure Principle* text was contradictory and impossible to understand. This is because we will only understand this text after having been through everything Freud says concerning the ego, from one end to the other of his work.

Beyond the Pleasure Principle, *Group Psychology and the Analysis of the Ego*, and *The Ego and the Id* are the three articles fundamental to the comprehension of the ego.

The normal (or not healthy) form of narcissism happens in professional or intellectual activities. Lacan addressed narcissism in his open sessions. You don't speak so you will be admired and recognized by others. The seminar is the place for the unseen and unexpected to manifest.

In the human order, we are dealing with the complete emergence of a new function, encompassing the whole order in its entirety. The symbolic function is not new as a function; it has its beginnings elsewhere than in the human order, but they are only beginnings. The human order is characterized by the fact that the symbolic function intervenes at every moment and at every stage of the subject's existence. In other words, the whole thing holds together. In order to conceive what happens in the domain proper to the human order, we must start with the idea that this order constitutes a totality. In the symbolic order the totality is called a universe.

The symbolic order from the first takes on its universal character. It isn't constituted bit by bit. As soon as the symbol arrives, there is a universe of symbols. The question one might ask – how many symbols, numerically, does it take to constitute the symbolic universe – remains open. But however small the number of symbols which you might conceive of as constituting the emergence of the symbolic function as such in human life, they imply the totality of everything which is human. The structure is a complete whole, which is together and complete [S (O)].

In ego psychology, the coherence is given by the synthetic function of the ego, rather than by the structure. For Lacan, first the Symbolic is a complete, total, unified structure, in which any element is differentially related to everything else. Later there will be a lack in the Symbolic, in language given by that there is no Other of the Other. The Name of the Father (O) functions as a stop gap of the lack in language to represent something of the Real that is beyond language. The ego as agent is coextensive with this completion of the structure; when the ego says I speak, the enunciating ego, this is the imaginary use of language.

In elementary structures, the rules of alliance are part of an extraordinarily rich, luxuriant network of preferences and prohibitions, of indications, of commands, of facilitations.

This symbolic order, since it always presents itself as a whole, as forming a universe all by itself – and even constituting the universe as such, as distinct from the world – must also be structured as a whole; that is to say, it forms a dialectic structure which holds together, which is complete.

This presupposes that the symbolic agencies function in the society from the start, from the moment it takes on a human appearance. The Symbolic is already there.

This is what is presupposed by the unconscious such as we discover and manipulate it in analysis – no distinction between descriptive and dynamic unconscious.

As machines rather than as animals, we possess greater freedom than animals who are fixed by the environment. Freedom means the multiplicity of possible choices, permutations, and combinations.

In its most essential aspect, the ego is an imaginary function. The fundamental, central structure of our experience really belongs to the imaginary order. And we can even grasp the extent to which this function is already different in man from what it is in nature as a whole. We rediscover the imaginary function in nature in the parade, so essential to sustaining sexual attraction within the species.

Now, in man the function of the ego possesses distinct characteristics. That's the great discovery of analysis – at the level of the generic relation, bound up with the life of the species, man already functions differently.

In man, there's already a crack, a profound perturbation of the regulation of life. That's the importance of the notion introduced by Freud of the death drive.

Freud wanted to save some kind of dualism at all costs. The ego, the libido, etc. – all of that was tending to produce a kind of vast whole, returning us to a philosophy of nature. The ego and Eros tend towards unity and synthesis.

This dualism is none other than what I am getting at when I emphasize the autonomy of the symbolic. The latter is an expression of the death drive for Lacan. Speech is mother to the misrecognized [*meconnu*] part of the subject, and that is the level peculiar to the analytic symptom – a level decentered in relation to individual experience, since it is that of the historical text which integrates it. The subject's life is oriented according to a problematic which isn't that of his actual experience, but that of his destiny, namely – what does his history signify!

What is at issue is determining whether, in analysis, this function of speech exerts its impact by substituting the authority of the analyst for the ego of the subject, or whether it is subjective. The order created by Freud demonstrates that the axial reality of the subject isn't in his ego. Intervening by substituting oneself for the ego of the subject, which is what is always done in one way of practicing the analysis of resistances, is suggestion, not analysis.

The symptom, whatever it may be, isn't properly resolved when the analysis is practiced without putting at the top of the agenda the question of ascertaining where the action of the analyst must be directed: at what point on the subject, if I can put it like that, he must aim. Aim not at reality, at better adaptation but at the unconscious, although the auxiliary ego of the analyst (Strachey) was geared towards supporting a non-defensive ego which could tolerate the unconscious and reconcile desire and the law, the id, and the super-ego.

The unconscious is the unknown subject of the ego, that it is misrecognized [*meconnu*] by the ego, which is *der Kern unseres Wesens*, 'the core of our being.' The core of our being does not coincide with the ego.

The ego isn't the I, it is something else, a particular object within the experience of the subject. Literally, the ego is an object – an object which fills a certain function which we here call the imaginary function. What about the ego, in this perspective? The ego really is an object. The body in pieces finds its unity in the image of the other, which is its own anticipated image – a dual situation in which a polar, but non-symmetrical relation, is sketched out.

Freud's research on the second topography was undertaken in order to put back in its place an ego (an unconscious ego) which had begun to slide back to its old position. Everything Freud wrote aimed at reestablishing the exact perspective of the eccentricity of the subject in relation to the ego.

What is the image in the mirror? The real object isn't the object that you see in the mirror. The image in the mirror is a phenomenon of consciousness as such. We have manufactured instruments which, without in any way being audacious, we can imagine to be sufficiently complicated to develop films themselves, put them away into little boxes, and store them in the fridge. Despite all living beings having disappeared, the camera can nonetheless record the image of the mountain in the lake, or that of the Cafe de Flore crumbling away in total solitude.

Consciousness occurs each time there's a surface such that it can produce what is called an image. That is a materialist definition of consciousness. An image – that means the effects of energy starting from a given point of the real – think of them as being like light, since that is what most clearly evokes an image in our mind – are reflected at some point on a surface, come to strike the corresponding same point in space.

So then! This is what I want you to consider as being essentially a phenomenon of consciousness, which won't have been perceived by any ego.

But, on the other hand, I am quite happy to admit that there is an I in it – the symbolic subject. I am explaining to you that it is in as much as he is committed to a play of symbols, to a symbolic world, that man is a decentered subject. Well, it is with this same play, this same world, that the machine is built. The most complicated machines are made only with words.

Speech is first and foremost that object of exchange, the world of the symbol which makes algebraic calculations possible. The machine is the structure detached from the activity of the subject. The symbolic world is the world of the machine. Then we have the question as to what, in this world, constitutes the being of the subject. This subject, really, is no one. How can the world of the machine be the world of subjectivity? Deleuze and Guattari called them objective schizoid machines.

Now let us suppose our machines to have some sound recording equipment and let us suppose that a loud voice, we can easily imagine that someone supervises their operation, the legislator intervenes so as to regulate the ballet which up until now was only a round which might lead to a disastrous end. What's being introduced is a symbolic regulation, of which the unconscious mathematical subjacency of the exchanges of the elementary structures gives us the schema. The comparison ends there, for we aren't going to make an entity of the legislator – that would be yet another idol.

Our deduction of the subject, however, demands that we locate this voice somewhere in the interhuman game. To say that it is the legislator's voice would doubtless be an *idolification*, albeit of a high, though characterized, order. Isn't it rather the voice which knows itself when it resounds no longer to be no one's voice, but that of the waves and the woods? Valery is speaking its language here. And shouldn't we perhaps in the end recognize it, this voice, as the voice of no one.

The tendency to union – Eros tends to unite – is only ever apprehended in its relation to the contrary tendency, which leads to division, to rupture, to a redispersion, most especially of inanimate matter. These two tendencies are strictly inseparable. No notion is less unitary than that. Let us go over it step by step.

The organism already conceived by Freud as a machine tends to return to its state of equilibrium; this is what the pleasure principle states. (Not because the pleasure principle has a disequilibrium built into it which is what causes the development of the ego, the reality principle, the constancy principle, and the secondary process.) Now, at first sight, this restitutive tendency is not clearly distinguishable in Freud's text, from the repetitive tendency which he isolates, and which constitutes his original contribution. So, we ask ourselves the following question: what distinguishes these two tendencies?

The paradoxical question of the similarity or difference between the two principles in question is also reflected in the notion of the repetition compulsion. In *Beyond the Pleasure Principle*, Freud also introduces the tendency to repeat problematic or traumatic situations as evidence of phenomena which would constitute an exception to the pleasure principle. But is this repetition the obsessiveness of a desire leading to destructive consequences or the obsessiveness of an anti-libidinal ritual? Is the repetition compulsion, the compulsion to repeat a past experience of satisfaction/trauma, a renewed attempt at pleasure/unpleasure? Or is it an attempt to bind mental excitations? Are we going around in a circle of suffering, the wheel of samsara? Or are we turning the wheel of Nirvana, the hermeneutic circle of meaning and enlightenment? As an alternative formulation, I postulate a distinction between two types of binding and unbinding, one type of attachment and detachment linked to the primary process and another to the secondary process.

From the beginning of Freud's work to the end, the pleasure principle is explained in the following way. When faced with a stimulus encroaching on the living apparatus, the nervous system is, as it were, the indispensable delegate of the homeostat, of the indispensable regulator, thanks to which the living being survives, and to which corresponds a tendency to lower the excitation to a minimum. To a minimum – what does that mean?

The minimum tension can mean one of two things, all biologists will agree: according to whether it is a matter of the minimum given a certain definition of the equilibrium of the system, or of the minimum purely and simply; that is to say, with respect to the living being, death. One then ends up defining the aim of the pleasure principle as the concrete dissolution of the corpse. That is to assume that the problem has been resolved, that is to confuse the pleasure principle with what we think Freud designated under the name of the death drive.

There is something which is distinct from the pleasure principle, and which tends to reduce all animate things to the inanimate – that is how Freud puts it: What does he mean by this? What obliges him to think that? Not the death of living beings. It's human experience, human interchanges, and intersubjectivity. Something of what he observes in man constrains him to step out of the limits of life. No doubt there is a principle which brings the libido back to death, but it doesn't bring it back any old way. If it brought it back there by the shortest paths, the problem would be resolved. But it brings it back there only along the paths of life, it so happens. The principle which brings the living being back to death is situated, is marked out behind the necessity it experiences to take the roads of life.

At the level of the nervous system, when there are stimuli, everything works, everything comes into action, the efferent, the afferents, so that the living being returns to a state of repose. That's the pleasure principle, according to Freud.

On the intuitive level, there is, isn't there, some discordance between the pleasure principle defined thus, and what pleasure evokes in the way of raciness. Every man runs after his lady – that's what it looked like until now.

This libido, isn't it something rather libidinous? People seek their pleasure. So, why is this expressed theoretically by a principle which states the following: what is sought is, in the end, the cessation of pleasure. But you can see that the direction the theory takes at this point goes exactly in the opposite direction to that of subjective intuition – in the pleasure principle. pleasure, by definition, is bent on its end. The pleasure principle – the principle of pleasure – is that pleasure should cease.

The reality principle is usually introduced with the simple remark that too much pleasure-seeking ends in all kinds of accidents – you get your finger burnt, you get the clap, you get your face smashed in. That is how we have the genesis of what is called human learning described to us. And then we are told that the pleasure principle is opposed to the reality principle. In our perspective that obviously acquires another meaning. The reality principle consists in making the game last; that is to say, in ensuring that pleasure is renewed, that the fight doesn't end for lack combatants.

The reality principle consists in husbanding our pleasures, these pleasures whose aim is precisely to end in cessation.

What is more, one discovers that the actualizations of instinct would not occur without a call from the environment, as they say, which stimulates and provokes the crystallization of forms, of behavior and modes of conduct. There is a convergence, a crystallization, here which gives us the feeling, however skeptical we may be, of a pre-established harmony, subject to be sure to all kinds of difficulties cropping up. The notion of learning is in some way incapable of being differentiated from the maturation of instinct.

At the point of a harmonious natural mode of organismic functioning, of maturity, there is an abyss, a fault, and this what we are in the process of looking for, with *Beyond the Pleasure Principle*.

This is why Lacan says that we cannot understand the ego without *Beyond the Pleasure Principle*: the death drive and the unconscious part of the ego, the unconscious law of discourse and the symbolic.

Man is always in the position of never completely understanding the law, because no man can master the law of discourse in its entirety.

The subject's life is oriented according to a problematic which isn't that of his actual experience, but that of his destiny, namely – what does his history signify! I have often underlined that already before his birth, the subject is already located not only as a sender, but as an atom of concrete discourse. He is in the chorus line of this discourse, he himself is a message. A message has been written on his head, and he is entirely located in the succession of messages. Each of his choices is a speech.

Speech is mother to the misrecognized [meconnu] part of the subject, and that is the level peculiar to the analytic symptom – a level decentered in relation to individual experience, since it is that of the historical text which integrates it. From then on, what is certain is that the symptom will only give in to an intervention interceding at this decentered level.

What is at issue is determining whether, in analysis, this function of speech exerts its impact by substituting the authority of the analyst for the ego of the subject, or whether it is subjective. The order created by Freud demonstrates that the axial reality of the subject isn't in his ego.

That is censorship in so far as there can never be any relation with the law in its entirety, since the law is never completely made one's own. Irreducible distance between the name of the father and of the son. The law and the symbolic father as a transcendent function. Censorship and super-ego are to be located in the same register as that of the law. It is the concrete discourse, not only in so far as it dominates man and makes all kinds of fulgurations appear, makes everything which happens, everything which constitutes discourse, but in so far as it gives man his own world, which we, more or less accurately, call cultural. It is in this dimension that censorship is located, and you can see in what way it differs from resistance. Censorship is neither on the level of the ego (Lacan writes the subject), nor on that of the individual, but on the level of discourse, in so far as, as such, it constitutes, all by itself, a full universe, and at the same time there is something irreducibly discordant about it, in every one of its parts. The symbolic Other is both complete and lacking, dispossessing or unfulfilling and completing. This is the source of the symbolic death, of symbolic castration, of the breach or gap in the midst of life. A symbolic ethics of the law as a function, rather than as a moral content or tendency.

Personality as a Subset of Mind

Let's start first by defining Mind as distinct from the ego although personality theory is also understood as a branch of psychology or of the theory of mind. It is important to stress that Freud had a theory of Mind, because otherwise the ego and the personality could simply be understood in behavioral terms as conditioned behavior or as an aggregate of stimulus and response packets under the heading of habits.

Personality for Jung was the social mask. For Lacan the person is *personat* or a personal sounding through or hearing (*Jouis*-Sense). Jung focused on sacred images, while Lacan focused on the Symbolic/Real sound. Now it is interesting that sound is linked to phenomenology and yet is one the most efficient structural causes that can be counted with one hand. What you see is not how you see it. A phenomenon is replaced by structure precisely in the moment of the suspension of non-essentials (*epoge*). Structure is a function of the essence which is emptiness.

Freud identifies the conscious part of the ego with the seat of reason. However, there is more than one type of reason, and this is something that Freud did not consider at least in a systematic way. The aspect of the ego that functions according to ego-representations, narcissistic investments, and aggressivity, conflicts with the impartiality associated with reason in science. But the awareness and pure intellect associated with preconscious perception of the external world would in fact be consistent with the principles of science. But the unconscious intellect also knows things intuitively. Nous or the unconscious intellect provide the axioms that then must be tested by consciousness. Fantasies or fictions are generated by the fantasized ego.

Lacan's new Ego, or subject of and in the Real, is a fourth-degree differentiation within narcissism. This is the rock of symbolic castration and the most difficult of narcissistic wounds: the symbolic father and phallus are also found to be lacking – a zero or a nothing. Once the illusions regarding the ideal father and the disillusions regarding the lack and limitations of the father have been cleared in the transference to the analyst, the father remains as an empty symbolic function but still a function, nonetheless. There is some similarity here with Jung's Self which is a Hindu concept, while Lacan's subject is similar to the Buddhist notion of no-self.

Finally, Lacan argued that the subject is an "answer of the Real" and not "an answer of the Other" or of the Symbolic. However, the autonomy of the subject is empty or devoid of any inherent meaning. It is only within the Imaginary that the ego imputes to itself the function or agency of generating new meaning. New meaning is generated within the Symbolic itself as a function of the interaction between the emptiness of the Real and of the subject, and the dynamic interaction between the elements of an open structure under on-going construction. You have to fly the plane while it is continuously being constructed and improved. You have to use the self although there is no-self. Conventional egos and professionals have a difficult time precisely doing this.

Bibliography

Bion, W. (1995). *Attention and Interpretation*. New York: Jason Aronson.
Bion, W. R. (1965). *Transformations*. London: William Heinemann.
Fink, B. (1997). *A Clinical Introduction to Lacanian Psychoanalysis*. Cambridge: Harvard University Press.
Freud, S. (1893–1895). *Studies on Hysteria*. New York: Avon Books, 1966.
Freud, S. (1914). On Narcissism: An Introduction. *SE*, 14, 67–102.
Freud, S. (1923). The Ego and the Id. *SE*, 19, 3–66.
Jakobson, R. (1990). *On Language*. Cambridge: Harvard University Press.
Kohut, H. (1966). Forms and Transformations of Narcissism. *Journal of the American Psychoanalytic Organization*, 14, 243–272.
Lacan, J. (1957). The Instance of the Letter in the Unconscious. In: *Ecrits*, translated by Bruce Fink. New York: Norton, 2006.
Lacan, J. (1958–1959). *El Deseo y su Interpretacion: Seminar VI*, edited by Oscar Masotta. Buenos Aires: Nueva Vision, 1970.
Lacan, J. (1959–1960). *The Ethics of Psychoanalysis: The Seminar, Book VII*, edited by Jacques Alain Miller, translated by Dennis Porter. New York: Norton, 1992.
Lacan, J. (1960). The Subversion of the Subject and the Dialectic of Desire. In: *Ecrits*, translated by Bruce Fink. New York: Norton, 2006.

Lacan, J. (1966–1967). The Seminar of Jacques Lacan. Book XIV. In: *The Logic of Phantasy*, translated by Cormac Gallagher from unedited French manuscripts. Unpublished. Accessed December 13, 2017.
Lacan, J. (1972–1973). Encore: The Seminar of Jacques Lacan, Book XX. In: *On Feminine Sexuality, the Limits of Love and Knowledge*. New York: Norton, 1998.
Lacan, J. (1975–1976). Book XXIII. In: *The Sinthome*. Cambridge: Polity Press.
Lasch, C. (1979). *The Culture of Narcissism*. New York: Warner Books.
Moncayo, R. (1998). *Evolving Lacanian Perspectives for Clinical Psychoanalysis: On Narcissism, Sexuation, and Jouissance in Psychoanalysis and Culture*. London: Karnac.
Moncayo, R. (2017). *Lalangue, Sinthome, Jouissance and Nomination*. London: Karnac.
Moncayo, R. & Romanowicz, M. (2015). Going Beyond Castration in the Graph of Desire: The Letter. *Irish Journal of Lacanian Psychoanalysis*, 58, Spring 2015, 31–58.
Nasio, J. D. (1992). *The Concept of the Subject of the Unconscious: Cinq Lecons sur la Theorie de Jacques Lacan*. Paris: Rivages, 1992.
Porge, E. (1997). *Los Nombres del Padre en Jacques Lacan*. Buenos Aires: Nueva Vision, 1998.
Roudinesco, E. & Badiou, A. (2012). *Jacques Lacan, Past and Present*. New York: Columbia University Press.
Winnicott, D. W. (1970). *The Maturational Processes and the Facilitating Environment: Studies in the Theory of Emotional Development*. London: Routledge.

8 The Symbolic and the Imaginary

For the ego, the image of his body is the principle of every unity he perceives in objects. Now, he only perceives the unity of this specific image from the outside, and in an anticipated manner. Because of this double relation he has with himself, all the objects of his world are always structured around the wandering shadow of his own ego. They will all have a fundamentally anthropomorphic character, even egomorphic we could say.

The object is always more or less structured as the image of the body of the subject. The reflection of the subject, its mirror image, is always found somewhere in every perceptual picture, and that is what gives it a quality, a special inertia. That happens when we see the subject substituted for by the polycephalic subject – this crowd made up of the imaginary plurality of the subject, of the fanning out, the blossoming of the different identifications of the ego. At first this seems to us like an abolition, a destruction of the subject as such. The subject transformed into this polycephalic image seems to be somewhat acephalic. If there is an image which could represent for us the Freudian notion of the unconscious, it is indeed that of the acephalic subject, of a subject who no longer has an ego, who doesn't belong to the ego. And yet he is the subject who speaks, for that's who gives all the characters in the dream their nonsensical lines – which precisely derive their meaning from their nonsensical character.

Well, approaching from a different angle, we come upon the same thing again – every imaginary relation comes about via a kind of you or me between the subject and the object. That is to say – If it's you, I'm not. If it's me, it's you who isn't. The struggle to the death between the master and servant. That's where the symbolic element comes into play. On the imaginary level, the object ever appear to manifest within relations that fade. He recognizes his unity in them, but uniquely from without. And in as much he recognizes his unity in an object, he feels himself to be in disarray in relation to the latter.

DOI: 10.4324/9781003509349-9

38 The Symbolic and the Imaginary

This disarray, this fragmentedness, this fundamental discordance, this essential lack of adaptation, this anarchy, which opens up every possibility of displacement, that is of error, is characteristic of the instinctual life of man – the very experience of analysis shows us that (the gap or lack in desire and the asymmetry between the sexes – jouissance). What is more, if the object is only graspable as a mirage, the mirage of a unity which can never be grasped again on the imaginary level, every object relation can only be infected with a fundamental uncertainty by it. That is in fact what so many different experiences show one and calling them psychopathological conveys nothing since they lie on a continuum with many experiences which themselves are regarded as normal.

That is where the symbolic relation comes in. The power of naming objects structures the perception itself. The percipi of man can only be sustained within a zone of nomination. It is through nomination that man makes objects subsist with a certain consistence. If objects had only a narcissistic relationship with the subject, they would only ever be perceived in a momentary fashion. The word, the word which names, is the identical. The word doesn't answer to the spatial distinctiveness of the object, which is always ready to be dissolved in an identification with the subject, but to its temporal dimension. The object, at one instant constituted as a semblance of the human subject, a double of himself, nonetheless has a certain permanence of appearance over time, which however does not endure indefinitely, since all objects are perishable. This appearance which lasts a certain length of time is strictly only recognizable through the intermediary of the name. The name is the time of the object. Naming constitutes a pact, by which two subjects simultaneously come to an agreement to recognize the same object. If the human subject didn't name – as Genesis says it was done in earthly Paradise – the major species first, if the subjects do not come to an agreement over this recognition, no world, not even a perception, could be sustained for more than one instant. That is the joint, the emergence of the dimension of the symbolic in relation to the imaginary.

In the dream there's the recognition of the fundamentally acephalic character of the subject, beyond a given point. This point is designated by the signifying structure of the dream or the movement of the signifier within its structure. That's where the I of the subject is at that moment, when the ego dissolves into a multiplicity of identifications, a voice which is nothing more than the voice of no one causes the signifier to emerge, as the last word on the matter, the word for everything. And this word means nothing except that it is a word.

Freud in his dream is already addressing himself to us. He is already dreaming for the community of psychologists, of anthropologists. It isn't

The Symbolic and the Imaginary 39

just for himself that he finds the alpha and omega of the acephalic subject, which represents his unconscious. On the contrary, by means of this dream it's him who speaks; that is to say while speaking to us something which is both him and no longer him. Here I am only the representative of this vast, vague movement, the quest for truth, in which I efface myself (Self-effacing Aphanisis, alienating and liberating at the same time). To the extent that I desired it too much, that I wanted to be the creator, I am not the creator. The creator is someone greater than I. It is my unconscious, it is this voice which speaks in me, beyond me. This analysis will now enable us to go further and understand how we should conceive of the death instinct, the death instinct's relation to the symbol, to this speech which is in the subject without being the speech of the subject.

The function of the death instinct, beyond the pleasure principle, which Freud introduces as being what governs the ego. (The pleasure principle governs both desire or the libido and the repressive principle.) Beyond the homeostasis of the ego, there exists a dimension, another current, another necessity, whose plane must be differentiated. This compulsion to return to something which has been excluded by the subject, or which never entered into it, the Verdrangt, the repressed, we cannot bring it back within the pleasure principle (repression side of the pl. pri). If the ego as such rediscovers and recognizes itself, it is because there is a beyond to the ego, an unconscious, a subject which speaks, unknown to the subject. We must therefore posit another principle. Why did Freud call it the death instinct? That's what we will try to get hold of in the encounters to come. The aphanisis of the subject (the ego) under the signifier is the work of the death drive (but this is not a destructive jouissance – it marks the appearance of the symbolic subject – the signifier).

Es (*Es*) is homophonous to the letter S, but it's also the unbarred subject, the analytic subject; that is to say not the subject in its totality. Unary trace. The part which contains the whole because everything is connected to everything else. People spend their time plaguing us about taking it in its totality. Why should it be a whole? We haven't the faintest idea. Have you ever encountered whole beings? Perhaps it's an ideal. I've never seen any. I'm not whole. Neither are you. If we were whole, we would each be in our corners, whole; we wouldn't be here, together, trying to get ourselves into shape, as they say. It is the subject, not in its totality, but in its opening up. As usual, he doesn't know what he's saying. To be sure, that isn't where he sees himself – that is never the case – even at the end of analysis. He sees himself in *a*, and that is why he has an ego.

What analysis teaches us, on the other hand, is that the ego is an absolutely fundamental form for the constitution of objects. In particular, it perceives what we call, for structural reasons, its fellow being, in the form of the specular other. This form of the other has a very close relation to the ego, which can be superimposed on it, and we write it as *a'*.

The imaginary gains its false reality, which nonetheless is a verified reality starting off from the order defined by the wall of language. The ego such as we understand it, the other, the fellow being, all these imaginary things are objects. When the subject talks to his fellow beings, he uses ordinary language which holds the imaginary egos to be real. In other words, we in fact address A, those we do not know, true Others, true subjects. They are on the other side of the wall of language, there where in principle we never reach them. Fundamentally, it is them I'm aiming at every time I utter true speech, but I always attain a', a", through reflection. I always aim at true subjects, and I have to be content with shadows.

The perverted inflection which analytic technique has been acquiring for some time is founded on wanting the subject (the ego) to gather everything which he experienced in the pregenital stage, his scattered limbs, his partial drives, the succession of partial objects. One wants to allow this ego to gather its strength, to realize itself, to integrate itself – the dear little thing. If this end is pursued in a direct fashion, if one focuses on the imaginary and the pregenital, one necessarily ends up in that sort of analysis in which the consummation of partial objects is achieved through the intermediary of the image of the other (yes, but this is the analyst occupying the place of the ego-ideal, not the ideal ego [*a-a'*]. The partial drive is reduced to the ego. The place of the agent in language, consciously identified with cultural norms – is the successful ego. I speak, therefore I am. The wall of language as the ego ideal is different than the aphanisis of the ego under the signifier, *lalangue*, where the place of the ego is left vacant, and autonomy is found not in the ego but in the symbolic itself). An ethics implied within language regardless of its moral content.

One trains analysts so that there are subjects in whom the ego is absent. That is the ideal of analysis, which, of course, remains virtual. There is never a subject without an ego, a fully realized subject, but that in fact is what one must aim to obtain from the subject in analysis.

The analysis must aim at the passage of true speech, joining the subject to another subject, on the other side of the wall of language. That is the final relation of the subject to a genuine Other, to the Other who gives the answer one does not expect, which defines the terminal point of the analysis. (The surprise, the unexpected, the unknown returns from the symbolic subject. Which is the other which is not an imaginary alter/rival or the subjective other of the unconscious.)

The analysis consists in getting him to become conscious of his relations, not with the ego of the analyst, but with all these Others who are his true interlocutors, whom he hasn't recognized. It is a matter of the subject progressively discovering which Other he is truly addressing, without knowing it, and of him progressively assuming the relations of transference at the place where he is, and where at first, he didn't know he was. (Are these the imaginary others of the dream, of the acephalic subject, or the subject of the signifier of the signifying structure?) The imaginary others as alter egos have to be deconstructed into signifying elements of the drive, the symbolic hate and love for the object.

There are two meanings to be given to Freud's phrase – *Wo Es war, Soll Ich werden*. Where Id was in the ideal ego, there ego should be, or I will become in the ego ideal. This *Es* we will take as the letter S. It is there, it is always there. It is the subject. At the end of the analysis, it is him who must be called on to speak, and to enter into relation with the real Others. Where the S was, there the Ich should be. Partial drives should be where the I was, because otherwise they will create symptoms.

The Ideal Ego

Elsewhere (Moncayo, 2008) I dedicated a chapter to differentiating four degrees within narcissism. In the first level, we find absolute and relative primary narcissism that include a state without a subject or object differentiation, and a narcissism of the object, however paradoxical this may sound; the ideal ego is the second degree of narcissism; the ego-ideal is the third. The fourth degree is associated with benevolent depersonalization, subjective destitution, and the traversal of the fantasy. While the first three are in Freud, the fourth degree is clearly associated with Lacanian theory and the end of analysis. The fourth degree coincides with what Lacan (1975–1976) calls a new ego in the Real. In addition, following Lacanian theory a clear conceptual distinction can be established between the ideal ego and the ego-ideal.

What I mean by narcissism of the object or of a narcissistic object is not what is usually considered to be a characteristic of a narcissistic personality and a fixation to the body image. For Lacanians this latter phenomenon represents a fixation to the ideal ego. The narcissism of the object refers to the object of fantasy even before there was an ego. In hallucinatory wish fulfillment, the fixation is with the *objet a* or the fantasy of the breast. This quality of the object of fantasy is used to describe a neonatal and early, if not primitive, form of mental functioning that continues throughout life as a modality of the imaginary sexual relation to the Other sex.

From the breast as an object cause of desire, to weaning and the separation from the breast to the acquisition of the body image as a replacement for the mother's gaze and breast, the image in the clear mirror represents the body image of the child as the child's own image but also as the object cause of the mother's desire. The child identifies with the object of the mother's desire, who or what she sees in the child that is not the child's but the mother's.

However, through the specular image the object becomes the child's own Ideal Ego (i[a]). Through the specular image the child acquires a bodily identity and a unified body image. The object of the drive is what transmits the drive to the ideal ego (a→a'). The representations of the drive appear as representations of the object. But what was chaotic, unconscious, and scrambled information about the unconscious object now becomes a unified body image that is two-dimensional. We can't see the back of our heads and yet we know the back is there and that we are three dimensional despite what the mirror says.

Lacan identifies the S (homophony with Es [Id or It] in German) of the pre-subject with the It. I argue that in the beginning the non-differentiation between subject and object represents 'It' and in a second moment (relative primary narcissism), the identification with the object breast represents the Id. In this formulation, it is important to remember that in the non-differentiation between subject and object, as seen in the example of intrauterine life, the subject and the object are still connected through the placenta that Lacan considers as one of the first *objet a*.

Absolute primary narcissism is a state wherein the libido is stored both in the It and in the S or pre-subject. In relative primary narcissism libido emanates from the object but also from the ego since the ego is identified with the object that is the first form of ego. In relationship to the breast, energy is sexualized and when the ego desexualizes object libido it is simply returning to the prior condition wherein energy emanates both from the pre-subject and the object.

Freud says the ego is a bodily ego which first means an organismic ego, and secondly, a body image that replaces the primary object. The body image is a two-dimensional surface reflected in a mirror (mother's eyes, water, metal surface, or modern clear mirror). But Freud also says the ideal ego is a mental projection of the surface of the body and a projection of the organism unto the mind. The body becomes the mind in the specular image or the ideal ego.

The ideal ego becomes a long-lasting structure of the subject, more than a pathological fixation that needs to be abandoned. The specular image becomes pathological if the lack in the image is not symbolized in the direction of the ego ideal.

The Ego Ideal

In the previous work mentioned, following Freud's idea of degrees of differentiation within narcissism, and Lacan's distinctions between the ideal ego and ego-ideal, I established a difference between the ideal ego constructed on the model of the relationship with the mother in contrast to the ego ideal that is constructed based on the relationship to the father/Other. The ideal in the ideal ego is a body image, while the ideal in the ego-ideal and the relationship to the father represents social and intellectual ideals (values, concepts, identifications). The ego ideal is a symbolic body of signifiers of the Other that the ego appropriates and invests with narcissistic libido with a + and − sign. The super-ego represents the − sign of the ego ideal.

As the ego-ideal provides new aims for narcissism, the super-ego embodies imaginary castration and narcissistic injuries. The ego-ideal now will mediate narcissism and self-love, self-respect, and pride. The Other and the ego-ideal will love the ego if the ego identifies with social ideals and complies with and develops good habits for ordinary living. Bad habits represent a defiance of the Other and a rejection of the symbolic castration and compliance/submission embodied in the ego ideal and good habits. The super-ego then will castigate (imaginary castration) the ego for the failure to uphold the ego ideals associated with the father and the Other.

The ego ideal can be identified with the narcissism and imaginary function of the Name of the Father (NoF) and its prestige. The NoF is the signifier, and the imaginary phallus is the signified as the object of the mother's desire. In development and symbolic castration, the child stops being the imaginary phallus of the mother and the imaginary phallus becomes the signified of the signifier of the NoF. The father is supposed to have the imaginary phallus that the mother wants, and its signifier is the NoF.

In this perceived move of the desire of the mother from the child to the father, the child goes from omnipotent fusion to castration/loss/separation. Lacanians speak of symbolic castration because the child loses the place of the imaginary object.

The child will then forward to the father the question of the missing object. What the child gets back from the father to compensate for the loss of the object (mother, *objet a*, imaginary phallus) is the NoF or the signifiers/ideals of the father/Other. The loss of the object is also a loss at the level of the ego. The pre-subject becomes the divided subject and the product of the division is the missing object/signifier. The object will always slide metonymically and thus cannot provide a stable identity for the subject. The NoF is what offers a stable metaphor that can stop the sliding and fracturing of the object.

However, the imaginary identification with the father and the imaginary function of the Name does not offer a stable solution to the ego either. It looks like the imaginary NoF can close the gap in the subject, but the narcissistic shine of the Name is always threatened by lack. The search for fame, stardom, fortune, power, etc. are all associated with the imaginary function/trappings of the NoF. These are all attempts to deny or close the lack in the subject. The NoF must move from the Imaginary to the Symbolic (in the sense of accepting the lack and castration in the father as symbolic rather than a real deficit) and from the Symbolic to the Real. In the move from the Symbolic to the Real, the Name reveals rather than conceals the lack while the void as Real acquires a different significance beyond symbolic lack.

The Ego in the Real

The move of the NoF (Name of the Father) from the Symbolic to the Real coincides with a further fourth-degree differentiation within the ego, from the ego-ideal to the ego in the Real. This is the rock of symbolic castration and the most difficult of narcissistic wounds: the symbolic father and phallus are also found to be lacking – a zero or a nothing. Once the illusions regarding the ideal father and the disillusions regarding the lack and limitations of the father have been cleared in the transference to the analyst, the father remains as an empty symbolic function but still a function, nonetheless.

The task of the analyst is to serve as a support for this function by ultimately being empty of content that could define the identity of the analysand. This is the exact opposite of what people ordinarily think the father function to be. The father function is typically associated with the super-ego and the ego-ideal, with telling people what to do and what not to do. Subjects, however, have to find out things for themselves and shape their own destinies based on the choices they make with the elements with which they are made. The Other cannot give the subject his or her own Being (Lacan, 1958–1959).

It is only with the fourth degree of differentiation within narcissism that the subject can rebirth itself (what Lacan calls *se-parere*) past imaginary ego-identifications. The subject is reborn as a new signifier that appears thanks to the autonomy and dynamic self-creating capacity of the Symbolic.

The Symbolic is autonomous or self-organized because it is capable of dynamic change over long periods of time. In addition, it is autonomous

The Symbolic and the Imaginary 45

from the subject because it conditions the subject rather than the other way around. On the other hand, the subject is autonomous from the Symbolic because it occupies the place of emptiness or a hole or a lack of closure within the structure. In this regard, the autonomy of the subject and the autonomy of the Symbolic seem to meet at this level. To produce a new signifier for the subject from the place where the Other cannot give the subject his or her own Being (the subject of the Real), the new signifier must emerge from the subject but also from the emptiness of the battery of signifiers or the lack in the Other. The lack in the Other, is the place within the Symbolic that gives access to the Real.

Finally, Lacan argued that the subject is an "answer of the Real" and not "an answer of the Other" or of the Symbolic. However, the autonomy of the subject is empty or devoid of any inherent meaning. It is only within the Imaginary that the ego imputes to itself the function or agency of generating new meaning. New meaning is generated within the Symbolic itself as a function of the interaction between the emptiness of the Real and of the subject and the dynamic interaction between the elements of an open structure under on-going construction.

In the analytical situation, the analyst functions from the place of suspended authority that represents this lack in the Other to define the identity of the subject. The subject is no longer fooled by the *objet a* that appears to fall off the Other but actually falls off from the place of the subject's own fantasy.

Paradoxically, the agency of the subject is limited to the act of leaving empty the place of ego-agency within the structure and the place of the cause of desire within the subject. On the other hand, the larger agency, the autonomy, and activity of the Symbolic could also represent the work of a benevolently depersonalized subject. The illusion is that the ego is the agent that advances and realizes things or symbolic causes but instead it is the Symbolic that advances and realizes the subject.

This is not unlike the work of the poet or the metaphoric subject who makes a non-instrumental use of language for new meanings and words to emerge from the Real as the locus of an essential void within the Symbolic. In the Greek myth of Narcissus, Narcissus drowns in a vain attempt to grab his image reflected in the water. But the story does not end there, because in a second moment, in the place where Narcissus fell, the narcissus flower appears. The narcissus flower represents the new subject.

The recognition of the emptiness of the Other, that Lacan symbolized in the image of the empty mirror without a fixed ego representation, also coincides with what Kohut (1977) called a cosmic narcissism marked not only by joy but also by a solemn and serene inner confidence. The emptiness of the mirror represents the calm and unperturbed nature of the mirror itself (Other jouissance). The mirror equally accepts, holds, and lets go of any image. What Lacan calls the calculated vacillation of the analyst's neutrality refers to this accepting and holding of the images and signifiers that appear in the mirror, but it also means letting them go, a quality that is classically associated with the analyst's neutrality. When the analyst holds the contents of the mirror, the emptiness of the mirror is still there.

Finally, what I am calling a fourth-degree or end-state narcissism is differentiated from first-degree primary narcissism (or the oceanic feeling, as Freud called it), because it includes rather than excludes all the mediations/separations introduced by the paternal function. End-state narcissism is not a primordial experience of identity with the mother, because within the Symbolic, identity is necessarily different or metaphoric.

Lacan argues that in the final analysis or in the end of analysis the *objet a* dissolves "owing to its failure, unable, as it is, to sustain itself in approaching the Real" (Lacan, 1971–1972, p. 95). When finally, the object is reached in the Real rather than the Imaginary, the object dissolves for this very reason. The mythical union with the One always produces 1+a. So how can the object vanish without producing a substitute as we just said happens with respect to the approach to the One?

In the case of Joyce, Lacan argues that in the new ego the image of the body is not involved. This contrasts with the ego in Freud that was a bodily ego but as a libidinal surface or image. Because we identify with the body image we relate to the other through the assumption of similar images, minds, and selves. Nietzsche (1885–1887) said something similar when he wrote, "The assumption of similar cases presupposes 'similar souls'" (p. 276). Soon these assumptions crystallize into concepts leading to the cognitive ego functions of affirmative judgments of attribution or negation: I am this, and you are not, or I am not that and you are this, or this is inside me and that is outside. However, the similarity of body image, racial features, gender, etc. points to the imaginary fact that the more similarity you find, the more difference you generate. The similarity or similitude based on the emptiness of the mirror and of the Other that we all share is something different.

At the end of analysis, the *i* (in the matheme i[a] for ideal ego) and the I (in matheme I[A] or I[O] for ego-ideal) can be detached from the *a* and the A/O respectively. This non-attachment signifies having ideas and ideals without idealization or imaginary identifications, to have a father ideal without an ideal father. The Imaginary is separated from the Real (i/a) and from the Symbolic (I/O), freeing the three registers to be re-articulated under the sinthome. The Real becomes the Real of the later Lacan: without the Imaginary of "the thing" and the fantasy of the imaginary phallus, the Imaginary becomes the creative Imagination, and the Symbolic contains the Real or where words hit the Real rather than cover it.

References

Kohut, H. (1977). *The Restoration of the Self*. New York: International University Press.

Lacan, J. (1971–1972). *The Knowledge of the Psychoanalyst*. London: Karnac.

Moncayo, R. (2008). *Evolving Lacanian Perspectives*. London: Karnac.

Nietzsche. F (1881). *The Will to power*. New York: Vintage Books.

The Seminar of Jacques Lacan. Book VI Desire and its interpretation, translated by Cormac Gallagher, http://www.lacaninireland.com/web/wp-content/uploads/2010/06/Book-06-Desire-and-its-interpretation.pdf. Accessed January 10, 2024.

9 The *Je* and the *Moi*, the Ego, and the Subject

The hole or lack in the Other (S [∅]), is the same as saying that there is a −1 inherent in the set of linguistic signifiers. Structurally this means that in speech there is a −1 or a missing signifier in every statement. Lacan (1960) says that this −1 is unpronounceable, but the operation can be pronounced whenever a proper name is pronounced in a statement. "The operation is the calculation of signification" as follows in the picture in Figure 9.1.

$$\frac{S(\text{signifier})}{s(\text{signified})} = s \text{ (the statement)},$$
with $S = (-1)$, we find: $s = \sqrt{-1}$
$$\frac{-1}{\sqrt{-1}} = -1$$

In the picture, the signifier is represented by −1 and the signified is represented as the square root of −1. When the signifier represents −1 and the signified represents square root of −1, the result of their division is −1. However, there is a double meaning to what the missing thing is. On the one hand, there is a missing signifier represented by −1, on the other hand, there is a signifier with no signified (the signified is not missing: it just does not exist, although it produces effects in speech).

Since Being is located inside the hole of the Other [∅], Lacan (1960) asks the question: "But where does this being, who appears in some way missing from the sea of proper names, come from?" (p. 694). The answer comes from the Real: "I am in the place from which the universe is a flaw in the purity of Non-being" (ibid). Birth and death require an impurity within the pure void or emptiness. Without impurity, nothing happens or Being does not manifest. The place of the I is the place of a flaw in the purity of Non-Being and this place Lacan also calls the place of

DOI: 10.4324/9781003509349-10

Jouissance (or the place of Life and Death, bodily pleasure, and pain). The I and jouissance share the lack of a signifier since the signifier is missing or is continually shifting. This is what Lacan calls the flaw in the purity of Non-Being. In the Other, beyond a simple and self-referential name or unary trace, there is a lack of a substantial and stable referential signifier for the subject.

It is interesting that Lacan says that the symbolic phallus is the signifier of jouissance, while the question of jouissance is "What am I?" Am I my mother's special object or do I have a symbolic identity that the Name and Word designates, or, furthermore, is this symbolic identity simply a signifier rather than an object of jouissance? Both the missing I or substantial subject and the symbolic phallus are signifiers of jouissance, yet jouissance is also said to not have a signifier and the signifiers themselves are missing. Since the signifier for the symbolic phallus is missing, more and more, jouissance cannot be defined neither by the object nor by the signifier. The subject becomes a trace of jouissance in the Real that, nonetheless, the subject still must take responsibility for. The I represents the subject of jouissance and the place where the I must take responsibility for jouissance and desire.

This traceless trace of jouissance is not only an energetic state but also a state of mind consciousness or of the Pcpt. Cs. system that does not retain impressions or representations of the subject or of the object. With respect to this singular trace all the subject can say or become is "This I am," or "I am this," or "Just this." Here "this" does not refer to the particular but to a singularity outside the signifier.

Does this correspond with the formula for sublimation that Freud gave in the Ego and the Id: "Where Id was, ego shall be"? No, because the ideal ego or ego-ideal are no longer objects of social utility or signifiers that close the gap in the subject. In the Lacanian graph of desire, the latter would translate into the upper signifying chain being expressed/concealed through the lower narrative of the ego and social discourses that give a tamed interpretation of the drive.

Lacan's (1959–1960) own formula and permutation of Freud's formula is: "Where It was, I shall become" (this or come to being). Lacan uses It instead of Id. By It he means a different concept of the Id. Instead of a chemical soup, chaos, or a seething cauldron of primitive impulses, the It is the "no-thing" as the nature of the object, jouissance, or *das Ding* in the Real as the subject qua-nothing. The Id instead refers to the 'thing' of the archaic object that framed the first form of ego wherein no boundaries between ego and object exist. The Id represents a form of malevolent depersonalization, in which the impersonal dimension of the drive determines the experience of the subject in the Real.

In the subject of the Real, the differences between subjects and signifiers is not lost, although the subject is in the gaps-in-between or outside the signifier, and inside the experience of jouissance. The 'no-thing' of the subject is not the same as the 'nothing' that is one of the *objet a*. The 'nothing' as the *objet a* represents the toxic absence of the object. The 'no-thing' is something different that contains both presence and absence and refers to the mystery of the letter and the Name wherein the I is benevolently depersonalized as a form of jouissance.

In addition, I would argue that the I here is the *Je* rather than the *moi* or ego. The *Je* is the subject of jouissance or the "Just This." In front of the image in the mirror of the Other, the subject or *Je* says: I am It, but it is not me. An analysand was bewildered and mildly disturbed by the growing realization in front of the mirror that, as he aged, he looked more and more like his father. He was concerned because he did not want to lose his sense of individuality and individuation.

By mirror of the Other I mean that a mirror is a product of culture while at the same time the empty mirror holds that which is undefined other than as a form of jouissance or energetic intensity. The specular image or ideal ego is me (*Je*) but I (*moi* – ego) am not It or I am not the image. The *Je* is not defined by the specular image but rather by the empty mirror and the pure capital signifier. Beyond name, language, culture, body, and body image, the question of "Who am I?" indicates/instantiates the place of jouissance.

A subject can also say, "My father is me, or his desire is mine, but I am not my father, and my desire is not his." My father defines my ego but not the *Je* or the I that remains indeterminate. There is something in me (*Je* or jouissance) that cannot be reduced to my father, but this is not the illusory autonomous ego associated with imaginary identifications. The *Je* of the unconscious is a singular empty place within the structure of the Other beyond the biographical father that represents a new place of permutation and transformation for the structure.

If the *Je* said, "I am my father, but my father is not me," the me in the second clause is granting autonomy to the father rather than the subject. The sign and value of the subject is not clear in the example. Assuming there are things in the ego that the subject values over and above the father, then the place of the lack would be in the Other rather than in the *Je*. This state of affairs is a pure form of alienation of the *Je* and of the son in the father represented by the super-ego in Freud's second theory of mind.

If the *Je* says, "I am not my father," then this opens the door to the *Je* of the S or a significant pure signifier in the Unconscious of a Real jouissance of both the Id and the It. In accessing the object of the drive beyond the father and the father's prohibition, the ego or the *moi* becomes the Id or the pure demand of the sexual drive or of phallic jouissance.

The *Je* of the signifier instead becomes a new signifier of identity that emerges from the Real of jouissance rather than from the ego or from a known battery of signifiers in the Other. This *Je* as It is not the Id, the super-ego/ego-ideal, or the ego; nor a simple summation of all three. The *Je* is a unary trace of the Pcpt. Cs. that does not retain ego representations in the Pcs-Cs system and therefore with the unary trace the signifier can be used both by awareness and the Unconscious without requiring the supposition of an ego supposed to know.

Reference

Lacan, J. (1959–1960). *The Ethics of Psychoanalysis*. London: Karnac.

10 Freud's and Lacan's Early Ego

Lacan wants to emphasize symbolic knowledge rather than a narcissistic display and competition among participants. Seminar II functions as an axis point between Freud and Lacan with vectors leading to various lines of development of Lacanian thought. But let us first explore Freud's thought.

According to Freud the secondary process and the ego arise out of the unsatisfying nature of hallucinatory and primary process experience. Freud depicted a primitive psychical apparatus regulated by an effort to avoid the accumulation of unpleasant excitation.

> Hypotheses, whose justification must be looked for in other directions, tell us that at first the apparatus's efforts were directed towards keeping itself so far as possible free from stimuli; . . . the exigencies of life confront it first in the form of the major somatic needs.
> (1900, p. 604)

This principle was first called by Freud the inertia principle but in *Beyond the Pleasure Principle* its name was changed to that of Nirvana principle. In addition, Freud distinguished between the Nirvana principle and the constancy principle. Although in *The Interpretation of Dreams* Freud utilized the constancy principle as the model for describing primitive mental functioning, I shall regard the Nirvana principle as the first principle due to the fact that Freud considered the constancy principle (the effort to reduce excitation and to maintain constant at the lowest possible level as opposed to abolishing it altogether [Nirvana]) as a secondary function, a second best option, a modification of the Nirvana principle required by the need for specific action in the world. Constancy represents life rather than radical annihilation.

The organism was seen as having to learn to tolerate a certain amount of energy required for the modification of the external world. Furthermore, since the need for specific action is not a primary event because

Freud also views the early organism as being incapable of specific action and of satisfying its own needs, it is more precise to regard the Nirvana principle as the original principle of mental functioning.

The principle of Nirvana is initially illustrated with what is commonly known as the model of a "reflex arc": the excitations received through the sensorial or perceptive end of the mind are promptly and totally discharged on the motor end. This concept is based on the essential postulate that an equal quantity of energy is supplied in one end to be reinstated in the form of movement in the other end. Nevertheless, in the earliest example of internal stimuli arising from somatic sources, this simple function sees itself interfered with by the fact that the child lacks the means for achieving a discharge of excitation via bringing about an experience of satisfaction. Freud equates discharge in the form of movement with the production of an internal modification and/or an expression of emotion.

Affectivity manifests itself essentially in motor (secretory and vasomotor) discharge resulting in an (internal) alteration of the subject's own body without reference to the external world. Motility in actions is designed to effect changes in the external world (1915, p. 179). Of course, internal motor discharge is not what most people think of feelings in a phenomenological sense.

The child moves in vain and cries helplessly attempting to fulfill the requirements of the zero principle according to the model of a reflex arc. The child cannot produce the movements necessary for need-satisfaction. Thus, the stimuli remain constant until the bodily balance has been reinstated. In intrauterine life, the internal modifications necessary for both the homeostasis of the nervous system (the discharge of excitation) and the satisfaction of bodily imbalances/needs were automatically regulated by virtue of the child still being a part of the mother's organism.

After birth the internal modifications can only be produced by the specific actions of the mother. Thus, the mother takes the place of the motor end of the mind and occupies an essential role in fulfilling the child's constancy principle. But since the realities of life inevitably introduce a breach in the stimulus/response activity composed of the child's bodily needs and the mother's actions, a "reflex apparatus" of a different sort comes into play.

Desire and the pleasure principle are originated qua insatiable because in the face of a return of somatic stimuli when the mother is absent, the child will attempt to lower the tension and satisfy the need by re-activating the mnemic image which most strongly was associated with a previous experience of satisfaction. "An impulse of this kind is what we call a wish" (1900, p. 605) and "the first wishing seems to have been a hallucinatory cathecting of the memory of satisfaction" (idem). That desire is insatiable simply means that it cannot be satisfied with any of the objects or persons in the real world.

Desire is a relation with a fantasized object and not with a real object independent from the subject. It is an attempt to reproduce a perceptual identity with a past and lost experience of satisfaction with the mother, through the cathecting of a rudimentary partial object memory which remained associated to it and as a primaeval vestige of that experience. Thus, the creation of hallucinatory wish-fulfillment coincides with the origin of desire and that of the primary process. Moreover, this state of affairs also marks the beginning of thought activity. "Thought is after all nothing but a substitute for a hallucinatory wish" (1900, p. 606).

Once desire is constituted within the regressive frame of ideational and imagenic hallucinatory wish-fulfillment under the primary process and the pleasure principle, it will forever remain trapped within the closed system of a reflex apparatus of the kind I have described. This "reflex apparatus" is of a different nature than the initial "reflex arc" reflecting the rule of the Nirvana principle. The motivational scheme of a stimulus which activates the elaboration of motor behavior as a means of obtaining an object of need-satisfaction which then culminates in the lowering of tension does not accurately describe the nature and function of desire within the mind. Desire qua insatiable is closer to the world of ideas, dreams, and fantasies than to a biological order of need-satisfying specific action in the external world. The memories of past experiences of satisfaction are stored in the unconscious and serve as inductive elements in the orientation of wishful thinking in both daydreams and dreaming during sleep (dream world).

Moreover, desire is insatiable or inexhaustible because fantasies, dreams, or ideas never fully produce the same result than an actual real experience of satisfaction. The eternal return of desire within a subjective world of ideas in the final instance always aims at reestablishing the identity with the first experiences of satisfaction with the mother. Since this, due to the incest prohibition and the requirements of separation and differentiation, is something impossible to accomplish in the real world, desire remains perennially unfulfilled.

With the maturation of motor activity and behavior through assimilation and adaptation (Piaget's definition of motor intelligence) to the conditions of the real world, more and more the child comes to learn a more efficient method for the discharge of internal excitation. The same way that under the pleasure principle the child appropriated the energy arising from somatic stimuli (which in the absence of the mother accumulated and became unpleasant) by binding it to the memories of acts of need-satisfaction, now he learns to withdraw the energy from the world of hallucinatory wishing and dream-like ideation (which also become unpleasant because the energy cannot be discharged or the desire satiated) in order to put it at the service of motor activity and specific action in the world. In addition, it should also be remarked that as Piaget has duly observed the development of motor activity and the orientation towards reality takes place within the context of coercive adult rules and social-moral behavior.

> From the hour of its birth certain regularities of conduct are imposed upon the infant by the adult, and, as we have shown elsewhere, every regularity observed in nature, every "law" appears to the child for a long time as both physical and moral.
>
> (1932, p. 88)

But within Freud's theory this inhibition of hallucinatory-satisfaction or ideational wish-fulfillment "becomes the business of a second system, which is in control of voluntary movement" (1900, p. 605).

Freud defines the preconscious system and the secondary process in similar terms. For the sake of effecting alterations in the external world, the mind needs to be able to make use of all the mnemic material laid down by experience. The preconscious becomes the portion of the mind which "succeeds in retaining the major part of its cathexis of energy in a state of quiescence and in employing only a small part on displacement" (1900, p. 638). In the preconscious the fact that each word retains its cathexis and is not displaced allows for a relatively stable store of memories, for reflection and reversibility and for preventing an unnecessary expenditure of energy. Contrary to this, in the unconscious, "by the process of displacement an idea may surrender to another its whole quota of cathexis"; while "by the process of condensation it may appropriate the whole cathexis of several other ideas." Freud proposes "to regard these two processes as distinguishing marks of the so-called primary psychical process" (1915, p. 186).

In *The Interpretation of Dreams* (1900) Freud defines censorship as the function of a second agency to which he attributes the essential task of excluding inadmissible ideas from consciousness.

> We have seen that we were only able to explain the formation of dreams by venturing upon the hypothesis of there being two psychical agencies, one of which submitted the activity of the other to a criticism which involved its exclusion from consciousness. The critical agency, we concluded, stands in a closer relation to consciousness than the agency criticized: it stands like a screen between the latter and consciousness. Further we found reasons for identifying the critical

agency with the agency which directs our waking life and determines our voluntary conscious actions.

(p. 579)

Freud goes on to describe the critical agency as "the preconscious" and the criticized system lying behind it as "the unconscious." At this point there has been a shift in Freud's thought. In his early clinical studies consciousness was the critical agency while now he accords this function to the preconscious system. Consciousness cannot be the seat of the critical moral faculty because in the mentioned work, Freud considers consciousness as a system (Cs.) occupying a lower position in the hierarchy of agencies. In Freud's view, consciousness is a kind of empty faculty without a content of its own and incapable of retaining mnemic traces. "We regard consciousness as a sense organ which perceives data that arise elsewhere" (idem, p. 179). Freud's whole metapsychology is built somewhat in contempt of what he regarded as the omnipotence of the pre-Freudian psychology of consciousness for which mind=consciousness. Thus, it follows from this that the preconscious and the critical faculty should also be unconscious in a descriptive sense.

Thus, there are two kinds of unconscious, which have not been distinguished by psychologists. Both of them are unconscious in the sense used by psychology; but in our sense, one of them, which we term the Ucs., is also inadmissible to consciousness, while we term the other the Pcs. because its excitations after observing certain rules – it is true and perhaps only after a fresh censorship, though nonetheless without regard to the Ucs. – are able to reach consciousness (S.E. 5:614).

The important point for this investigation is that the preconscious and censorship – a name Freud also uses to describe the critical faculty – stand like a screen between the Ucs. and consciousness but yet their own content can be subject to a fresh censorship. This observation is consistent with a distinction advanced by Freud in Section V of *The Unconscious* (1915) between two kinds of censorship: one situated between the Ucs. and the Pcs., the other between the Pcs. and consciousness.

The secondary process is set up to cathect ideas with bound energy so as to be in a position to inhibit any development of unpleasure which may proceed from them.

But the question arises of the different mode of operation on the part of the "second system" in the case of repression/censorship and in the case of establishing the secondary process. In the first case an inadmissible idea turned unpleasant is repressed, avoided, held back from the Pcs. system. In the second case an unpleasant idea is cathected in such a way that its energy is qualitatively modified; a difference in procedure which permits the unpleasant idea to remain in consciousness. This specific difference demonstrates the inadequacy of viewing repression or censorship as the function of the preconscious system and the secondary process. Freud himself will abandon this view in favor of his realization of the unconscious nature of repression and the fact that repression should be seen as a failure of the secondary process.

To the extent that repression emanates from the preconscious ego and opposes wishful impulses which press towards free discharge under the primary process, repression seems to be differentiated from the primary process and come closer to the secondary process and the ego's tendency towards the inhibition of primary psychical processes. But to the extent that repression produces the formation of symbols and substitute ideas it approximates the rule of the primary process at work in the unconscious.

Something has been added to A which has been subtracted from B. The pathological process is one of displacement, such as we have come to know in dreams – a primary process, therefore (1895, p. 350).

So, what is this aspect of repression which seems to express the nature of the unconscious primary process? In my opinion this point has never been sufficiently clarified within psychoanalytic theory. The primary process and the unconscious encompass antimonial and contrary phenomena. Since the dualism of a primary and secondary process does not coincide with the dualism of a repressed and a repressive tendency and both of the latter forces fall on the side of the primary process, then it follows that the first system has to encompass the conflict between the two aforementioned parties. From the point of view of the pleasure-unpleasure principle, desire and repression are the same thing. Because of the tendency to avoid unpleasant thoughts at work in the unconscious, the unconscious is unable to do anything but wish. Both repression and desire work under the pleasure-unpleasure principle.

The Nirvana principle constitutes a non-dual concept in Freud's theory given that, wittingly or unwittingly, Freud attributes to it both the tendency of the pleasure principle to seek satisfaction and avoid dissatisfaction and the tendency of defenses to reduce, contain, or organize the tensions, excitations, and pain produced by the pleasure principle.

Is there a difference between the repressed unconscious and repression itself as an unconscious process? What kind of unconscious is the unconscious of the repressive force? It has always been clear that repression pertains to an unconscious process and that it is the function of analysis to make conscious what has been repressed. But the confusion lies in whether repression pertains to an unconscious process in the sense that the unconscious implies repression or in the sense that repression itself is unconscious. In the latter case, the task of making conscious the unconscious would imply making conscious not only the repressed unconscious but also what I would call the repressive unconscious.

Part of this confusion between the repressed and the repressive unconscious is based on the fact that the notion of repression appeared at the beginning of Freud's discourse correlated to the concept of the unconscious.

As I will show shortly, the unconscious was seen as structurally dependent upon the concept and action of repression. This was true right up until the introduction of the idea of a supposedly unrepressed unconscious part of the ego. From then on Freud's theory acquired a more evolutionistic and developmental bent. He spoke of the mental agencies as succeeding one another in temporal stages.

Jacques Lacan made a point of emphasizing what he considered to be the scientific superiority of Freud's topographical metapsychology despite the personality theory provided by *The Ego and the Id*. In his view, *The Ego and the Id* was a theoretical-ideological retrogression on Freud's part. Lacan champions what he believes to be the structural nature of the Freudian metapsychology. In his theory and in that of the French structuralist movement, a structure refers to the synchronic and simultaneous interdependence elements within a totality. In Freud's first theory of the mind, the unconscious and the preconscious were created in one blow by the action of repression. It follows from this notion that repression and the unconscious would appear in correlation to one another in most Freudian texts prior to the second topography.

The distinction between preconscious and unconscious activity is not a primary one but comes to be established after defense has sprung up. Only then the difference between preconscious ideas, which can appear in consciousness and reappear at any moment, and unconscious ideas which cannot do so gains a theoretical as well as a practical value (1915, p. 26).

In *The Ego and the Id* (1923) Freud introduces the concept of an unconscious part of the ego in order to reconcile the two propositions that repression emanates from the ego and is unconscious. The important point to notice here is that the characteristic of repression being unconscious is not explained according to the results of repression being unconscious (due to the magnetic pregnancy or centripetal force of repressed ideas) but in terms of repression emanating even from the very start from an unconscious part of the ego. So I shall now proceed to examine the light which the so-called structural theory sheds on the theory of repression.

Freud believed the unconscious part of the ego to be different from the repressed unconscious.

> We have come upon something in the ego itself, which is also unconscious, which behaves exactly like the repressed – that is which

produces powerful effects without itself being conscious and which requires special work before it can be made conscious.

(Freud 1915, p. 17)

The clinical data that patients in the work of analysis are unaware of their resistances and of the nature of their failure to at times proceed with the work of free association plus the existence of an unconscious sense of guilt and the correlated notion of an unconscious self-critical faculty, led Freud to formulate the concept of an unconscious part of the ego.

But the question immediately arises: how can I differentiate the repressed unconscious from the unconscious part of the ego? Freud's silence on this matter is very striking; especially since he declares that the unconscious part of the ego behaves exactly like the dynamic repressed unconscious. Freud even uses for this new unconscious the same abbreviation (Ucs.) he reserved for the repressed unconscious.

> We recognize that the Ucs. does not coincide with the repressed it is still true that all that is repressed fs Ucs., but not all that is Ucs. is repressed. A part of the ego, too and Heaven knows how important a part – may be Ucs., undoubtedly is Ucs. And this Ucs. belonging to the ego is not latent like the Pcs., for if it were, it could not be activated without becoming Cs., and the process of making it conscious would not encounter such great difficulties.
>
> (p. 18)

Freud only asserts that not all that is unconscious is repressed although the case in point, the Ucs. part of the ego, behaves just as the repressed unconscious. It produces powerful effects without itself being conscious which reminds one of the systematic unconscious that works at a distance from consciousness and determines the production of symptoms. By the same token, one encounters resistances in making it conscious which implies a dynamic unconscious that remains unconscious because there is a contrary force blocking it from becoming conscious.

Freud does not give a systematic definition of the unconscious part of the ego or of how this concept is similar to or different from the repressed unconscious. He leaves the issue of the relationship between these two senses of the term unconscious enshrouded in obscurity. Moreover, everything that Freud says about the unconscious of the repressive force makes it seem as if it were repressed.

But before I advance further in my analysis of the unconscious of repression, I would like to recapitulate what Freud has said about the source of repression prior to *The Ego and the Id*. In *The Studies of Hysteria*

(1895) he observed that repression was the result of the incompatibility between the single idea that is to be repressed and "the dominant mass of ideas constituting the ego" (1895, p. 135).

Repression takes place because sexual ideas are incompatible with ethical standards. It follows then that ethical standards during this period were associated with consciousness, with effort, will, intentions, and the dominant mass of ideas constituting the ego.

Then in his paper *On Narcissism* (1914) Freud wrote:

> We have learnt that libidinal instinctual impulses undergo the vicissitude of pathogenic repression if they come into conflict with the subject's cultural and ethical ideals. Repression, we have said, proceeds from the ego; we might say with greater precision that it proceeds from the self-respect of the ego . . . We can say that the one man has set up an ideal by which he measures his actual ego . . . For the ego the formation of an ideal would be the conditioning factor of repression.
>
> (p. 93)

In *The Interpretation of Dreams*, the critical agency was attributed to the preconscious system (Pcs.). In *The Unconscious* (1915) these two views are synthesized under the concept of censorship as being the function of the system Cs. (Pcs.). Thus, we find two contrasting views in Freud: an impersonal or transpersonal, structural, or systemic view, and a personalistic ego view. In addition, we find an energetic or neurobiological view and a hermeneutic or symbolic view. Lacanian psychoanalysis articulates the structural with the symbolic perspective whereas ego-psychology articulates a personalistic symbolic perspective which leaves out the structuralist or transpersonal perspective.

The alternative is not between biological reductionism and a social personalism of Cs. and ego-based, intentional purposiveness. The Lacanian school offers a structural hermeneutic order coextensive with Freud's understanding of symbolic processes. Meanings, purposes, and intentions are neither synonymous with consciousness nor ego-functioning. Such assumptions show that Klein and Schafer have not seriously studied or understood Freud's *The Interpretations of Dreams* (1900) in which these categories were invoked to describe unconscious psychical processes.

It should also be remembered that a concept of intentionality derived from Husserl's phenomenology would not propose that "every act of the mind is essentially directed toward, aimed at, or oriented to a social other in the lower case" (Meissner, p. 207). The doctrine of intentionality specifies that consciousness is always consciousness of something. Here something represents an object rather than another. A better way of restating the same proposition is that consciousness is always conditioned by an object. This takes the ego element of autonomy and volition out of the concept of consciousness. The other does occupy a central place in the psychical structure of the subject but this other is not a fellow human subject. Rather, the other of intersubjectivity needs to be understood as mediated by the structure of the Ucs. as well as the symbolic social order of language, society, and kinship.

In *The Interpretation of Dreams*, when examining the role played by dream-thoughts in the construction of dreams, Freud borrows the notion of unconscious purposive ideas from Edward von Hartmann. If one establishes a self-evident equation between intentional and purposive ideas then one has to grant the fact that intentional might not only be a characteristic of consciousness.

Conscious intention and purposive ideas need to be distinguished from intentional purposiveness in the unconscious. The latter is better accounted for in terms of a signifying wish or the operation of unconscious desire according to the rule of the signifier. The signifier expresses both desire and the law. Conscious intention and purposive ideas need to be thought of as a function of the ego-ideal which has a role to play in the act of repression. Then how does one differentiate between the ethics of the ego-ideal and the ethics of the subject, of desire and the desire of the analyst. The latter is a second-order desire for knowing, emancipation, and signification.

On the personal side Freud defines the components of censorship as being "an attitude of condemnation," an "ethical, aesthetic or social point of view," and/or things we view with abhorrence due to the restraints imposed by morality. In *The Ego and the Id* Freud also regards the ego as the agent of censorship, with the exception that now he sees repression as emanating from an unconscious part of the ego.

Accustomed as we are to taking our social or ethical scale of values along with us wherever we go, we feel no surprise at hearing that the scene of the activities of the lower passions is in the unconscious; we expect, moreover, that the higher any mental function ranks in our scale of values the more easily it will find access to consciousness offered to it. Here however, psychoanalytic experience disappoints us. In our analyses we discover that there are people in whom the faculties of self-criticism and conscience – mental activities, that is, that rank as extremely high ones – are unconscious, and unconsciously produce effects of the greatest importance (p. 26).

Thus, two of the main themes of repression – that it emanates from the pole of ethical ideals within the ego and from an unconscious part of the ego – converge upon the concept of an unconscious source of ethics within the ego.

Freud conceives of a connection between repression, the unconscious part of the ego and between repression and the faculty of self-criticism and conscience. Repression seems to emanate from both sources. Freud also, as seen earlier, associates the unconscious with the faculty of self-criticism and the latter with the function of the super-ego. Thus, as I expect to show, Freud attributes the task of repression to both the unconscious part of the ego and to the super-ego. And he never defines the unconscious part of the ego nor does he ever establish a systematic relationship between the super-ego and the unconscious ego.

At the beginning of section II of *The Ego and the Id* after having introduced the concept of an unconscious part of the ego, Freud goes on to define the purpose of the work in question in the following way:

> Pathological research has directed our interest too exclusively to the repressed. We should like to learn more about the ego, now that we know that it, too, can be unconscious in the proper sense of the word.
> (p. 19)

I take this statement of purpose to mean that in *The Ego and the Id* Freud wants to concern himself with the nature of the repressive force. Part of this focus is meant as a response to the criticism that in his theory of the mind he did not deal with the higher strata of human nature. So, he wants to respond to what he thinks is an unjust reproach by deepening his understanding of repression, especially since he feels that he always addressed man's higher nature by from the very start attributing the function of instigating repression to the ethical and aesthetic trends in the ego.

Freud reduces the sublime to the principle of repression. In the same way that he oscillates between identifying repression with the secondary process, with the civilized mind, and with the primary process or the primitive mind.

But it is curious to me how Freud will concern himself with the study of the unconscious part of the ego as it pertains to the study of the repressive force. After the opening statement that I have quoted he continues to analyze the different ego functions such as the role of the ego in the act of perception and in relation to the external world, but he says nothing about the unconscious part of the ego. He himself realizes this when after defining the ego in terms of its relations to the Pcpt. Cs. and Pcs. systems he writes, "But, as we have learnt, the ego is also unconscious" (p. 23). However, once again instead of defining the unconscious part of the ego he moves on to introduce the concept of the id.

> I propose to take it into account by calling the entity which starts out from the system Pcpt. and begins by being Pcs. the 'ego,' and by

following Groddeck in calling the other part of the mind, into which this entity extends, and which behaves as though it were Ucs., the Id.

(p. 23)

Thus, the ego extends into an id which "behaves as though it were unconscious." If the id only behaves as if it were unconscious, it would seem that the unconscious Freud is here referring to cannot be the repressed unconscious. In a similar way the unconscious within the ego behaves exactly like the repressed though it is not repressed. Therefore, in the course of recognizing that the ego is more than the Pcpt. Cs. (Pcs.) system and in order to explain this other unconscious part of the ego, Freud interpolates the notion that the id is the region of the mind which extends beyond the reality surface of the ego. In my opinion Freud is here implying (later he will say it explicitly) that the unconscious repressive force (Ucs. ego) is either a part of and/or arises from the id. Just as earlier Freud wrote that there can be an unrepressed unconscious, he now writes that although the repressed merges into the id, it is only a part of it. The unrepressed portion of the id appears to at least share several important characteristics with the unconscious part of the ego.

Therefore, it is my contention that Freud advances the concept of the super-ego precisely to explain the relationship between an unconscious self-critical faculty, the unconscious part of the ego and the id.

> If the ego were merely the part of the id modified by the influence of the perceptual system, the representative in the mind of the real external world, we should have a simple state of things to deal with. But there is a further complication. The considerations that led us to assume the existence of a grade in the ego, a differentiation within the ego, which may be called the "ego ideal" or "super-ego," have been stated elsewhere. They still hold good. The fact that this part of the ego is less firmly connected with consciousness is the novelty which calls for explanation. [No italics]
>
> (p. 28)

At this juncture I see six theoretical elements coming together within Freud's theory. Firstly, the notion that repression emanates from the ego; secondly, that repression is connected to a critical faculty (censorship); thirdly, that repression is unconscious; fourthly, that repression emanates from an unconscious part of the ego; fifthly, that the unconscious part of the ego is the part of the ego which extends into the id; and finally that the super-ego or ego-ideal, which had been identified with the ethical and critical agency that serves as the conditioning factor for repression (*On Narcissism*), now can be inferred to be the part of the ego which extends into the id and is less firmly connected with consciousness. In other words, the super-ego is the part of the ego which extends into the id and is unconscious though not repressed in Freud's view.

The abundant communication between the ideal and these Ucs. instinctual impulses solves the puzzle of how it is that the ideal itself can to a great extent remain unconscious and inaccessible to the ego.

(p. 39)

Therefore, I feel it is plausible to conclude that at least an aspect of the super-ego is the unconscious source of morality and repression within the ego. It is my contention that Freud never systematically defined the unconscious part of the ego as being the source of repression. He merely asserted that this unconscious of the ego or of the repressive force differs from the repressed unconscious in that it is not repressed. However, he did not explain why an unconscious which is not repressed remains incapable of consciousness. In his metapsychology Freud had made a distinction between a latent unconscious and a repressed unconscious, and defined the unconscious due to repression as conformed by those mental contents which remain persistently and systematically outside the sphere of consciousness.

In point of fact everything Freud says about the unconscious part of the ego – other than his assertion to the contrary – makes it seem as if it were repressed. But instead of further defining the unconscious part of the ego, the problems posed by this concept take him to introduce the concepts of the id and the super-ego. Yet, Freud never explicitly acknowledged that the super-ego was the product of the inquiry into discovering the nature of the unconscious part of the ego. He comes close to this when he observes that the communication between the super-ego or the (moral) ideal and the id solves the puzzle of how morality (the ideal) as the source of repression can remain unconscious and inaccessible to the ego.

References

Freud, S. & Breuer, J. (1895). *Studies on Hysteria*. New York: Avon Books.
Freud, S. (1895). *Project for a Scientific Psychology*.
Freud, S. (1900). *The Interpretation of Dreams*. London: Hogarth Press.
Freud, S. (1914). *On Narcissism: Vol. 4 of the Standard Edition*. London: Hogarth Press.
Freud, S. (1915). *The Metapsychology: Vol. 14, vol. 4 of the Standard Edition*. London: Hogarth Press.
Freud, S. (1923). *The Ego and the Id: Vol. XIX of the Standard Edition*. London: Hogarth Press.
Piaget, J. (1932). *The Moral Judgement of the Child*. London: Routledge.

11 The Self in Winnicott and Kohut

Winnicott, as is well known, refers to the Self to the experience of the child in receiving empathy and good-enough mothering. Because the child feels loved by the mother, he can explore and love the world. These feelings are the true self. But love is not enough, since caretakers can experience love; it is the mother's desire that is fundamental. This is what Lacan called the jouissance of and with the (m)Other.

But for Lacan this was an inconvenient state that needs to be overcome with separation, and the transitional object helps along with it. But the relation to the object is facilitated by the father not the mother. But Lacan missed the *Madonna col bambino* feeling, that is buttressed by the invisible Name of the Father. This is the healthy self that is a no-self since it's made of other non-self-elements.

The false self is not a fake persona or mask, or narcissism, like in Freud and Jung, but is the false self the child develops to please the mother and be loved. This is the compliant or pleaser self without the submission that goes with the Name of the Father.

Kohut also focuses on early Oedipal development that he calls the pre-Oedipal, rather than the first phase of Oedipus as Lacan does. He differentiates between undifferentiated self-object fantasy relations, and a differentiated reality relationship between subject and object in which the object is independent from the subject. Kohut sees no function for the father in this object world, or language, and also does not distinguish among biological need, behavioral demand, and psychical desire.

12 Uses of the Concept of the Individual in Psychoanalysis

Finally, are the differences among the different concepts of the individual in the different schools of psychoanalysis ontological or epistemological? In other words, is it just a question of the concept, or of the word used by each school, or is there a true definition yet to be discovered for the individual, and the others should be rejected as ideological?

The concept of self should be rejected as non-existent because there is no self. However, there is a concept of no-self and does this exist? If no-self self-existed as an entity, then that no-self would be the same as a self. So, no, no-self is not a self. What is no-self on the one hand is the interdependent of the structure, and on the other hand it is the experience of emptiness in and by the subject. So, the concept of self is replaced by the concept of emptiness and interdependence, just as the concept of self in psychoanalysis is replaced by the concept of the unconscious and also of emptiness.

The concept of the subject does not imply that the subject is an entity. The subject is only a signifier or the word in language when a human being speaks. In this sense we could say that the concept of the subject is true. However, are words true? Is a word knowledge? Perhaps words could be knowledge if they were handled as concepts rather than words, as in science.

Knowledge is on a different side than the question of truth. Knowledge is not the same as truth. Truth is knowledge verified. One may have knowledge, but not true knowledge, not scientific knowledge, which not only requires statistics. Truth requires the experience of jouissance outside the signifier. Truth is not only objective, requiring numbers, probabilities, and statistics, but also subjective while being emotionally neutral, yet compassionate. Subjectivity is not the same as subjective bias.

Thus, I conclude that the subject is a true category despite not appearing as human and personal as the concept of the person. A person is not sound and has a mask or a face that may be true or untrue. There is something intimate and 'spiritual' about the term personal that is Real and not

DOI: 10.4324/9781003509349-13

Imaginary like the mask or the ego. The contradiction is reconciled with the subject of jouissance and various levels of jouissance that take the subject to evolved forms of jouissance and enigmatic meaning.

In psychosis there is no differentiated ego, only a schizoid subject or false self. In normality this is the first phase of individual development, but the psychotic individual does not proceed further. Due to the rejection of the intervention of the father, the psychotic does not accede to a coherent use of language and therefore their thought is fragmented and characterized by loose associations. For psychosis classical analysis is contraindicated. The schizoid subject remains subjugated to the Other as an object.

The normal condition is the divided and suffering subject that remains attached and clinging to the imaginary ego. In the case of the ideal ego, the image of the ego is what of the mother the ideal ego has appropriated. The desire of the mother is the basis for the Winnicottian good-enough mothering and the true self. Is also the basis for the self-object emphatic attunement of Kohutian analysis. The Kohutian analyst is a mother that tacitly becomes a father to help the analysand grow into differentiated subject-object relations.

The most common condition is that patients in psychotherapy complain of not having been loved by their mothers and fathers. This experience is not differentiated from an Oedipal rejection, in which the analysand felt rejected by the mother's love and desire for the father. In addition, in China, for example, individuals cannot distinguish between feeling unloved and the parents obeyance to Confucian values not to teach desire to their children.

13 The Ego or Subject of the Real

There is the pre-ego that was unified with the mother's body and infinite life before birth. This Real body becomes the imaginary body of the ideal ego in the mirror that identifies the mirror and its reflection as the mother's desire.

The imaginary ego then is denied by the bar that creates a barred subject and symbolic subject that is identical to the signifier ($). But the subject of the Real, or the Sinthome, creates an accord for a new subject of infinity: 8. This could be seen as continuous with the oceanic feeling of the body experienced as water, as a body reflected in the water. The oceanic feeling is what Freud understood as the Hindu concept of blessed feeling that is experienced with the mother at the breast. Nevertheless, this oceanic feeling has to be lost for separation and differentiation to take place under the father, and for a language to be established that cannot be unlearned.

The mystic oceanic feeling is not the same as the oceanic feeling with the mother. The mystic feeling includes the separation provided by the father. The union with the symbolic father includes separation.

Bibliography

Fink, B. (1997). *A Clinical Introduction to Lacanian Psychoanalysis*. Theory and Technique. Cambridge: Harvard University Press.
Freud, S. (1893–1895). *Studies on Hysteria*. New York: Avon Books, 1966.
Freud, S. (1914). On Narcissism: An Introduction. *SE*, 14, 67–102.
Freud, S. (1923) The Ego and the Id. *SE*, 19, 3–66.
Jakobson, R. (1990). *On Language*. Cambridge: Harvard University Press.
Kohut, H. (1966). Forms and Transformations of Narcissism. *Journal of the American Psychoanalytic Organization*, 14, 243–272.

Lacan, J. (1957). The Instance of the Letter in the Unconscious. In: *Ecrits*, translated by Bruce Fink. New York: Norton, 2006.

Lacan, J. (1958–1959). *El Deseo y su Interpretacion: Seminar VI*, edited by Oscar Masotta. Buenos Aires: Nueva Vision, 1970.

Lacan, J. (1959–1960). *The Ethics of Psychoanalysis: The Seminar, Book VII*, edited by Jacques Alain Miller, translated by Dennis Porter. New York: Norton, 1992.

Lacan, J. (1960). The Subversion of the Subject and the Dialectic of Desire. In: *Ecrits*, translated by Bruce Fink. New York: Norton, 2006.

Lacan, J. (1966–1967). The Seminar of Jacques Lacan: Book XIV. In: *The Logic of Phantasy*, translated by Cormac Gallagher from unedited French manuscripts. Unpublished. Accessed December 13, 2017.

Lacan, J. (1972–1973). Encore: The Seminar of Jacques Lacan, Book XX. In: *On Feminine Sexuality, the Limits of Love and Knowledge*. New York: Norton, 1998.

Lacan, J. (1975–1976). Book XXIII. In: *The Sinthome*. Cambridge: Polity Press.

Moncayo, R. (1998). *Evolving Lacanian Perspectives for Clinical Psychoanalysis: On Narcissism, Sexuation, and Jouissance in Psychoanalysis and Culture*. London: Karnac.

Moncayo, R. (2017). *Lalangue, Sinthome, Jouissance, and Nomination*. London: Karnac.

Romanowicz, M. & Moncayo, R. (2015). Going Beyond Castration in the Graph of Desire: The Letter. *Irish Journal of Lacanian Psychoanalysis*, 58, Spring 2015, 31–58.

Roudinesco, E. & Badiou, A. (2012). *Jacques Lacan, Past and Present*. New York: Columbia University Press.

Index

Adorno, T. 6
alliance, rules of 27
altruism 19, 26
androgyny 21
Assagioli, R. 6
Atheism 1
authority 15, 16, 19; of analyst 28, 32; figures 24; internal 16; parental 15, 24; suspended 45

Being 1, 45, 49; *see also* Non-Being
Big Self 22
Bion, W. R. 23
Bionian Infinite 22
bisexuality 16, 21
blessed feeling, Hindu concept of 71
Buddha, Shakyamuni 1
Buddhism 1; *see also* Chan Buddhism

capitalism 7
Cartesian *cogito ergo sum* 23–24
castration 43; imaginary 43; symbolic 21, 33, 43, 44
censorship 9, 13, 32–33, 56–58, 61–62, 64
Chan Buddhism 1
China 7, 70
Christ 3
collective unconscious 21
compassion 5, 69
complex: inverted 16; positive 16
Confucian values 70

consciousness 3, 6, 9, 24–25, 29, 33, 50, 56–58, 59–62, 64–65; ego 22, 25; self- 19, 22
constancy principle 30, 53–54
Copernican revolution 24
culture(s) 24, 51; European 5; German language 19; Indian 5; one-based 5; Romance language 19; zero-based 5

Dasein 3
death drive 17, 26, 28, 31–32, 39
Deleuze 29
depersonalization 41, 50
desire(s) 3, 9, 13, 14, 16, 17, 22–24, 26, 28, 30, 38, 39, 41–43, 45, 50, 51, 54–56, 58, 62, 67, 70, 71; analyst's 62; erotic 16, 26; heterosexual 16; homosexual 16; mother's 24, 42, 43, 67, 71; object of 3, 16; psychical 67; sexual 16; unconscious 9, 62
dialectics 6–7, 25, 27; dialectical logic 6; Hegelian 6; Marxist 7; negative 6
dreams 9, 37–39, 41, 55–58, 62; *The Interpretation of Dreams* 53, 56, 61–62

ego 1, 3, 5, 9–11, 13–17, 19–20, 21–30, 32–34, 37–47, 49–65, 70; -agency 3, 45; auxiliary 28; bodily 42, 46;

consciousness 22; Freud's Early 53–65; -identification 15; imaginary 23, 40, 44, 70, 71; Lacan's Early 53–65; -libido 26; of narcissism 25–33; non-defensive 24, 28; pre- 71; preconscious 58; in the Real 44–47; *The Ego and the Id* 17, 26, 50, 59–60, 62–63; unconscious 13–14, 28, 63; *see also* Ego; ego ideal; ego-psychology; ideal ego; super-ego
ego ideal 3, 9, 10, 15, 40–44, 64
egoism, 19, 26
ego-psychology 19, 22, 24, 61
empiricism 19
Eros 5, 17, 19, 2628, 30
erotic desires 16, 26
ethics 22, 33, 40, 62
existence 3, 9, 26, 60, 64
existentialism 3

father function 44
Freud, S. 3, 5–6, 9–10, 13–17, 19, 21, 24–26, 28–33, 38, 39, 41–43, 46, 50, 51, 67, 71; *Beyond the Pleasure Principle* 26, 30, 32, 39, 53; Early Ego of 53–65; *The Ego and the Id* 17, 26, 50, 59–60, 62–63; *Group Psychology and the Analysis of the Ego* 26; *The Interpretation of Dreams* 53, 56, 61–62; *Mourning and Melancholia* 14; *On Narcissism* 61, 64; *The Studies of Hysteria* 60; *Totem and Taboo* 17; *The Unconscious* 57, 61; *see also* dreams; ego; Freudian theory; id; narcissism; Oedipus complex; pleasure principle; super-ego; Unconscious, the
Freudian slips 23
Freudian theory 25

Groddeck 64
Guattari, F. 29

hedonism 26
Hegel, G. H. 6
Heidegger, M. 3; *see also* Dasein
heterosexual 16–17
Hinduism 1, 34, 71
homosexual 16
humanism 3
Husserl 3, 61

id 9–10, 11, 14, 16–17, 19, 26, 41, 50–52, 59, 62–65
ideal ego 24, 40–43, 46, 50, 51, 70, 71; *see also* ego ideal
identifications 3, 14–17, 19, 24, 37, 38, 42–44, 46, 51; father 16, 17, 15–17, 44; imaginary 44, 46, 51; imaginary ego- 44; mother 16–17; primary 15; super-ego 15
identity 21, 42–46, 50, 52, 55; bodily 42; perceptual 55; stable 43; symbolic 50
idol 29
idolification 30
imaginary, the 1, 3, 21, 23, 24, 27, 28, 34, 37–47
incest 15, 16, 55
individual 15, 21, 24, 25, 28, 32; liberal theories of 5–7; social structural theories of 5–7; uses of concept of in psychoanalysis 69–70
inertia principle 53
instinct 26, 32, 38, 39, 61, 65
intentionality 3, 23, 61
intersubjectivity 31, 62
It, the 42, 50

Je 21, 51–52
Jesus 119
jouissance 1, 6, 7, 20, 38–39, 46, 50–52; absolute 6; phallic 6, 52; Other 1, 6, 46; relative 6

Jung, C. G. 21–22, 33, 34
Jungian theory of the Self 21–22

kinship 62; rules of 24
knowing 41, 62; intuitive 22;
    'unknowing-' 22; 'unknown' 6
knowledge 1, 6, 69; antithesis 6;
    dialectical 6; scientific 69; self-
    22; symbolic 53; synthesis 6;
    thesis 4; true 69; unconscious 22
Kohlberg 19
Kohut, H. 45, 67

Lacan, J. 1, 3, 5, 7, 13, 15, 22,
    23–24, 26–28, 32–34, 41–46,
    49–50, 53–65, 67; Early Ego
    of 53–65; *see also* Sinthome
Lacanian Subject 23–34
Lacanian thought 1, 53
language 13, 23–24, 27, 30, 40,
    45, 51, 67, 69–71; German 19;
    Mandarin Chinese 1; Romance
    19; rules of 24; social 23;
    symbolic social order of 62;
    wall of 40
liberal theories 5–7
libido 15, 26, 28, 31, 39, 42; ego-
    26, 28; narcissistic 15, 42, 43;
    object 15, 26, 42
logic: dialectical 6; formal 6
love 5, 17, 23, 41, 43, 67, 70;
    agape 5; asexual 5; eros 5, 17,
    19, 26, 28, 30; passionate 25;
    self- 25, 43; 'Universal' 5

Madonna col bambino 67
Mandarin Chinese (language) 1
Marx, K. 3
Marxism 3; dialectic 7
masculinity 16
mind 1, 3, 9, 13, 21, 24, 29,
    42, 46, 50, 54–57, 59, 64;
    civilized 63; personality as
    subset of 33–34; preconscious/
    descriptive unconscious
    24; primitive 63; repressed
    unconscious 24; *see also*
    consciousness; mind, theory of;
    psyche
mind, theory of 13, 21, 33, 63
moi 23, 49–52
morality 10, 19, 62, 65
mothering, good-enough 67, 70
motor intelligence 55
mystic feeling 71

name 23, 27, 50–51; proper 49;
    self-referential 50; *see also*
    Name of the Father (NoF)
Name of the Father (NoF) 23, 27,
    32, 43, 44, 67
naming 38
narcissism 24, 41–44, 67;
    absolute primary 42; cosmic
    45; degrees/levels of 33, 41;
    ego of 24–33; end-state 46;
    first-degree primary 46; of the
    object 41; *On Narcissism* 61,
    64; relative primary 41–42
Narcissus 45
nature 3, 5, 6, 10, 14–16, 27, 28,
    45, 50, 53, 55, 56, 58–60, 63,
    65; human 63
nervous system 30, 31, 54
Nietzsche 46
Nirvana principle 53–55, 58
Non-Being 1, 49–50
non-self 67; Hindu 1
no-self 1, 22, 34, 67, 69

object cathexes 14–16
'objectification' 3
objective schizoid machines 29
oceanic feeling 46, 71
Oedipal rejection 70
Oedipus complex 9, 14–15, 17
One, the 1
Other, the 3, 5–7, 9, 13, 21–29,
    33–34, 39, 40, 41, 43–46,
    49–52, 53, 54, 56, 57, 61, 62,
    64, 65, 67, 69, 70; hole of 45;
    sex 41

parental figures 24
Peirce, C. S. 7
person 3, 15, 19, 21, 55, 62, 67, 69; phenomenology of 3
personality 13; narcissistic 41; as subset of mind 33–34; theory 33, 59
personal unconscious 21
phallus 23, 33; imaginary 43, 47; symbolic 50
phenomenology 33, 61; of Person 3
philosophy 1, 25, 28
Piaget, J. 56
Plato 5
pleasure principle 26, 30, 31, 39, 54–55, 58; *Beyond the Pleasure Principle* 26, 30, 32, 39, 53; *see also* pleasure-unpleasure principle
pleasure-unpleasure principle 58
possession 25
pragmatism 19
preconscious 9, 33, 56–59, 61
pre-ego 71
primary process 22, 30, 53, 55, 58, 63
psyche 3, 6, 21
psychoanalysis 1, 3, 6, 17, 19, 61, 69–70
psychopathology 9
psychosis 9, 70
psychosynthesis 6

quantum theory 6

Real, the 1, 6, 23–25, 27, 29, 33, 34, 40, 41; Ego in 44–47; subject of 45, 51, 41
reality principle 30–32
Real unconscious 23
reason 10, 14, 15, 16, 19, 22, 33; seat of 33
reflex arc 54–55
religion 1
repressed-repressive unconscious 9–11

repression 9–10, 13–14, 17, 39, 57–65; theory of 59
Ricoeur 16
Rimbaud 24

secondary process 9, 30, 53, 56–58, 63
self, the 34; compliant/pleaser 67; concept of 21, 69; eternal 1; false 67, 70; Hindu 1; Jungian theory of 21–22; in Kohut 67; in Winnicott 67; *see also* Big Self; non-self; no-self; self-image
self-image 23
semiosis 7
sexual drive 14, 26, 52
Sinthome 23, 46, 71
social norms 3
social structural theories 5–7
soul 1, 46
speech 3, 21, 28–29, 32, 39–40, 49
Spirit 6
structural theory 13–17, 59
subject, the 1, 3, 6, 7, 9, 13, 17, 19, 21–34, 37–45, 49–52, 54–55, 57, 61, 62, 67, 69–71; concept of 69; Lacanian 23–34; of the Real 45, 51, 71; *see also* subjectivity
subjectivity 22, 24–25, 29, 69; inter- 31, 62
sublimation 9, 17, 50
super-ego 9–11, 13–17, 19, 28, 32, 43–44, 51, 52, 63–65; unconscious 10–11
suppression 9
Symbolic, the 6, 9, 13, 19–20, 21, 23–24, 26–29, 32–34, 37–47; *see also* symbolic identity; symbolic phallus
symbolic identity 46, 50
symbolic phallus 50

Thanatos 26
truth 6, 26, 39, 69

unconscious, the 3, 6, 9, 13–14, 21–25, 37, 39, 51–52, 55–65, 69; conscious 11; ego 10–11, 14, 22, 62; intellect 33; part of the ego 10, 32, 59–60, 62–65; Real 23; super-ego 10–11; *The Unconscious* 57, 61; *see also* Bionian Infinite; collective unconscious; personal unconscious; repressed-repressive unconscious

Winnicott, D. W. 67, 70
word(s) 1, 24, 26, 29, 38, 40, 45, 47, 50, 56, 63, 65, 69

zero principle 54

Milton Keynes UK
Ingram Content Group UK Ltd.
UKHW031328071224
451979UK00004B/24